BaptistWayPress®

Adult Bible Study Guide

1 and 2 Kings

Leaders and Followers—Failed and Faithful

Bob Campbell
Perry Lassiter
Ron Lyles

BaptistWayPress®
Dallas, Texas

1 and 2 Kings: Leaders and Followers—Failed and Faithful—Adult Bible Study Guide

Copyright © 2008 by BAPTISTWAY PRESS®.
All rights reserved.
Printed in the United States of America.

No part of this book may be used or reproduced in any manner whatsoever without written permission except in the case of brief quotations. For information, contact BAPTISTWAY PRESS, Baptist General Convention of Texas, 333 North Washington, Dallas, TX 75246–1798.

BAPTISTWAY PRESS® is registered in U.S. Patent and Trademark Office.

Scripture marked NIV is taken from The Holy Bible, New International Version (North American Edition), copyright © 1973, 1978, 1984 by the International Bible Society. Used by permission of Zondervan Publishing House. Unless otherwise indicated, all Scripture quotations are from the New International Version.

Scripture marked NRSV is taken from the New Revised Standard Version Bible, copyright 1989, Division of Christian Education of the National Council of the Churches of Christ in the United States of America. Used by permission. All rights reserved.

Scripture marked NASB is taken from the New American Standard Bible®, Copyright © The Lockman Foundation 1960, 1962, 1963, 1968, 1971, 1972, 1973, 1975, 1977, 1995. Used by permission.

BAPTISTWAY PRESS® Management Team
Executive Director, Baptist General Convention of Texas: Charles Wade
Director, Missions, Evangelism, and Ministry Team: Wayne Shuffield
Ministry Team Leader: Phil Miller
Publisher, BAPTISTWAY PRESS®: Ross West

Cover and Interior Design and Production: Desktop Miracles, Inc.
Printing: Data Reproductions Corporation
Cover Photo: Mount Carmel, bibleplaces.com

First edition: March 2008
ISBN–13: 978–1–934731–03–1

How to Make the Best Use of This Issue

Whether you're the teacher or a student—
1. Start early in the week before your class meets.
2. Overview the study. Review the table of contents and read the study introduction. Try to see how each lesson relates to the overall study.
3. Use your Bible to read and consider prayerfully the Scripture passages for the lesson. (You'll see that each writer has chosen a favorite translation for the lessons in this issue. You're free to use the Bible translation you prefer and compare it with the translation chosen for that unit, of course.)
4. After reading all the Scripture passages in your Bible, then read the writer's comments. The comments are intended to be an aid to your study of the Bible.
5. Read the small articles—"sidebars"—in each lesson. They are intended to provide additional, enrichment information and inspiration and to encourage thought and application.
6. Try to answer for yourself the questions included in each lesson. They're intended to encourage further thought and application, and they can also be used in the class session itself.

If you're the teacher—
A. Do all of the things just mentioned, of course. As you begin the study with your class, be sure to find a way to help your class know the date on which each lesson will be studied. You might do this in one or more of the following ways:
   - In the first session of the study, briefly overview the study by identifying with your class the date on which each lesson will be studied. Lead your class to write the date in the table of contents on page 7 and on the first page of each lesson. *Note:* **An Easter lesson is included for classes or groups using these materials during the Easter season. If your class uses the Easter lesson, you may need to decide how to study the other lessons, such as by combining two lessons or studying the missed lesson at a special class meeting.**
   - Make and post a chart that indicates the date on which each lesson will be studied.

1 AND 2 KINGS: *Leaders and Followers—Failed and Faithful*

- If all of your class has e-mail, send them an e-mail with the dates the lessons will be studied.
- Provide a bookmark with the lesson dates. You may want to include information about your church and then use the bookmark as a visitation tool, too.
- Develop a sticker with the lesson dates, and place it on the table of contents or on the back cover.

B. Get a copy of the *Teaching Guide*, a companion piece to this *Study Guide*. The *Teaching Guide* contains additional Bible comments plus two teaching plans. The teaching plans in the *Teaching Guide* are intended to provide practical, easy-to-use teaching suggestions that will work in your class.

C. After you've studied the Bible passage, the lesson comments, and other material, use the teaching suggestions in the *Teaching Guide* to help you develop your plan for leading your class in studying each lesson.

D. You may want to get the additional adult Bible study comments—*Adult Online Bible Commentary*—by Dr. Jim Denison, pastor of Park Cities Baptist Church, Dallas, Texas, that are available at www.baptistwaypress.org and can be downloaded free. An additional teaching plan plus teaching resource items are also available at www.baptistwaypress.org.

E. You also may want to get the enrichment teaching help that is provided on the internet by the *Baptist Standard* at www.baptiststandard.com. (Other class participants may find this information helpful, too.) Call 214–630–4571 to begin your subscription to the printed edition of the *Baptist Standard*.

F. Enjoy leading your class in discovering the meaning of the Scripture passages and in applying these passages to their lives.

Writers of This Study Guide

Bob Campbell, the writer of units 1 and 2, lessons 1–4, and the Easter lesson, is retired after forty-seven years of ministry. He last served as pastor of Westbury Baptist Church, Houston, Texas. In addition to other pastorates, Dr. Campbell was professor of Bible at Howard Payne University, Brownwood, Texas. He has served as president of the Baptist General Convention of Texas. He is a graduate of Louisiana College and Southwestern Baptist Theological Seminary (B.D., Th.D.).

Perry Lassiter is a veteran curriculum writer who has served as a pastor for more than forty-five years. Now semi-retired, he continues to serve as an interim pastor. For thirty of his years as a pastor, he also taught Sunday School classes. He wrote unit 3, lessons 5–8. He is a graduate of Baylor University and Southern Baptist Theological Seminary, and he lives in Ruston, Louisiana.

Ron Lyles, pastor of South Main Baptist Church, Pasadena, Texas, wrote units 4 and 5, lessons 9–13. Dr. Lyles is a graduate of Dallas Baptist University and Southwestern Baptist Theological Seminary (M. Div., Ph.D.). He has taught adjunctively for Houston Baptist University and for the Logsdon School of Theology. In 2006, he was honored as "Citizen of the Year" by the Chamber of Commerce of Pasadena.

1 and 2 Kings: Leaders and Followers—Failed and Faithful

How to Make the Best Use of This Issue — 3

Writers for This Study Guide — 5

Introducing 1 and 2 Kings: Leaders and Followers—Failed and Faithful — 9

Date of Study

UNIT ONE
The (Supposed) Glory Days

LESSON 1 — *The Right Place to Begin*
1 Kings 2:10–12; 3:1–15 — 17

LESSON 2 — *Prayer to a God Who Keeps Promises*
1 Kings 8:22–36, 41–51 — 25

UNIT TWO
The Broken Kingdom

LESSON 3 — *A Leader's Foolish Choice*
1 Kings 12:1–20 — 37

LESSON 4 — *So Bad So Soon*
1 Kings 15:9–19; 16:29–33 — 47

UNIT THREE
Prophets at Work

LESSON 5 — *A Call to Full Commitment*
1 Kings 18:1–2, 17–39 — 57

LESSON 6 — *Time to Listen*
1 Kings 19:1–18 — 67

LESSON 7 — *Speaking Truth to Power—Alone*
1 Kings 22:6–28 — 77

1 AND 2 KINGS: *Leaders and Followers—Failed and Faithful*

| LESSON 8 | _____ | *Extending God's Help to a "Foreigner"*
 2 Kings 5:1–19a | 87 |

UNIT FOUR
Missing the Last Chance

| LESSON 9 | _____ | *Drifting Toward Disaster*
 2 Kings 14:23–29; 15:8–10, 13–14, 17–30 | 99 |
| LESSON 10 | _____ | *Death of a Nation*
 2 Kings 17:1–18, 21–23 | 109 |

UNIT FIVE
Missing the Last Chance: The Sequel

LESSON 11	_____	*When the Situation Is Desperate* 2 Kings 18:1–19, 29–31; 19:1–11, 14–20	121
LESSON 12	_____	*The Only Hope* 2 Kings 22:1—23:4	133
LESSON 13	_____	*The Bitter End* 2 Kings 23:31–32, 36–37; 24:8–9, 18–20; 25:8–21	143
EASTER LESSON	_____	*"Do Not Be Afraid"* Matthew 28:1–10	153

Our Next New Study	161
Future Adult Studies	162
How to Order More Bible Study Materials	163

Introducing

1 AND 2 KINGS:
Leaders and Followers—Failed and Faithful

A Perspective for Getting the Most Out of 1 and 2 Kings

Take your Bible and open it to 1 Kings. Notice the first person mentioned in the very first verse of the very first chapter. It's David, right? David, of course, was Israel's second king. David reigned about 1000–961 B.C.

Although David succeeded King Saul, David took first place over Saul in the hearts of the people. Indeed, David took first place over *all* the kings of Israel. Even though David was far from perfect, the people revered him as their greatest king. As 1 Kings 15:5 states, "David had done what was right in the eyes of the LORD and had not failed to keep any of the LORD's commands all the days of his life—except in the case of Uriah the Hittite."[1] Even David's adultery with Bathsheba and his murder of Uriah could not knock David from the pedestal on which the nation put him.

As we study 1 and 2 Kings, we will see David's shadow at various places, for he was the ideal earthly king whom the Hebrews yearned they would have again but never did. The story told in 1 and 2 Kings is largely one of failed leadership—unbelievably and tragically so for a nation whom God had chosen to serve him.

Now turn to the last few verses of the very last chapter of 2 Kings. Notice the person mentioned there, the one who was king of Judah. It's Jehoiachin, a name likely not nearly as familiar to you as that of David. Jehoiachin reigned over Judah briefly in 598 B.C. As David was the second king from the beginning, Jehoiachin was the second king from the end, at least as earthly kings go.

Jehoiachin really was more of a puppet than a king, though. The true ruler can be found in the next name in the last few verses of 2 Kings, "King Evil-merodach of Babylon" (2 Kings 25:27). Chances are you

1 AND 2 KINGS: *Leaders and Followers—Failed and Faithful*

know this person not at all. Ironically, though, the place to begin in order to understand 1 and 2 Kings is with him, or at least in Babylon.

We will help ourselves in getting the most out of 1 and 2 Kings if we realize that these books were Judah's attempt to understand why their nation had been defeated and destroyed and most of the people had been carted off to Babylon. The final destruction of the nation by the Babylonian army occurred in 587 B.C. In their agony, the people asked, *Why did this happen? How could it have happened? What had gone so horribly wrong that it had happened?* The answers to such questions are in 1 and 2 Kings.

Although we call these books *historical books*, we would do well to realize that they are at least as much theological in nature as they are historical. These books want us to see Israel's history from a distinct angle. That angle is called *deuteronomic theology*. Simply put, deuteronomic theology says that blessing comes when people obey God's instruction and punishment comes when people disobey. This bedrock truth was the guide for understanding Israel's history. So these books focus on this question from the perspective of the people in Exile: *Why was Israel (the Northern kingdom) utterly destroyed, wiped from the face of the earth, never to return, and why was Judah (the Southern kingdom) then destroyed and taken into Exile?* The answer of deuteronomic theology was that the people—leaders and followers alike—had sinned, and 1 and 2 Kings tells the sometimes gory details of how this occurred.

Additional Resources for Studying 1 and 2 Kings:[3]

A. Graeme Auld. *I and II Kings*. The Daily Study Bible. Louisville, Kentucky: Westminster John Knox Press, 1986.

Walter Brueggemann. *1 & 2 Kings*. Smyth & Helwys Bible Commentary. Macon, Georgia: Smyth & Helwys, 2000.

John Gray. *1 & 2 Kings: A Commentary*. Revised Edition. Old Testament Library. Philadelphia: Westminster Press, 1970.

M. Pierce Matheney, Jr., and Roy L. Honeycutt, Jr. "1 and 2 Kings." *The Broadman Bible Commentary*. Volume 3. Nashville, Tennessee: Broadman Press, 1970.

Richard D. Nelson. *1 and 2 Kings*. Interpretation: A Bible Commentary for Teaching and Preaching. Louisville, Kentucky: John Knox Press, 1987.

Choon-Leong Seow. "The First and Second Books of Kings." *The New Interpreter's Bible*. Volume III. Nashville: Abingdon Press, 1999.

Introducing 1 and 2 Kings: Leaders and Followers—Failed and Faithful

Where These Books Fit in the Bible

The Books of 1 and 2 Kings are in a set of books that the Hebrews called *the prophets*. Jewish leaders saw the Hebrew Bible as having three major divisions—*the law, the prophets*, and *the writings*. *The law* consists of the first five books of the Bible—Genesis, Exodus, Leviticus, Numbers, and Deuteronomy. *The prophets* includes the *former* prophets and the *latter* prophets. The *latter* prophets are what we call the prophetic books—books like Isaiah, Jeremiah, and the rest of the prophets. The *former* prophets are what we sometimes call the *historical* books—Joshua, Judges, 1 and 2 Samuel, 1 and 2 Kings. The former prophets were named *former* simply because they were placed before the latter prophets in the Hebrew Bible.

Israel considered that the books in both the former and the latter prophets were needed to understand the events that had happened during the long stretch of history they cover—about 700 years. In Israel's view, the former prophets, including the Books of 1 and 2 Kings (which cover about 400 years), dealt with a message similar to that of many of the prophets, just in another way.

The message of these books was valuable in understanding why such bad things had happened to God's people. The Northern kingdom had been destroyed in 722 B.C. The Southern kingdom had been destroyed and taken into Exile in 587 B.C. Why had this happened? The short answer is that they brought it on themselves by living in disobedience to God. Furthermore, if they wanted to keep it from happening again, they must obey God and not follow the path of the failed leaders and followers described in 1 and 2 Kings.

So the former prophets—the Books of Joshua, Judges, 1 and 2 Samuel, and 1 and 2 Kings—consider the history of Israel from this theological point of view. The focus is not simply on events but on the *meaning* of those events. The focus is particularly on what those events told about God's call and Israel's response down through the centuries.

The Hebrew book, by the way, is simply Kings. The idea for 1 and 2 Kings came about as a practical matter when the ancient Greek translation of the book, the Septuagint, put the books in two scrolls instead of one. It's all one account, one story, one theological treatise.[2]

1 AND 2 KINGS: *Leaders and Followers—Failed and Faithful*

What About Us?

We will study these materials best if we ask what they have to teach us as we study each lesson. Although these books are not New Testament books, we can still learn much from them.

Perhaps the largest area of instruction has to do with our own responsiveness to the Lord. What do the bad leaders have to teach us about what *not* to do? Too, what do the few good leaders teach us about what *to* do? Our belief in the God of grace whom Jesus most clearly has revealed to us does not mean God no longer holds people—and leaders and nations—accountable for their actions. We, too, are accountable to God.

UNIT ONE. 1 KINGS 1—11 THE (SUPPOSED) GLORY DAYS (1 KINGS 1—11)

Lesson 1	The Right Place to Begin	1 Kings 2:10–12; 3:1–15
Lesson 2	Prayer to a God Who Keeps Promises	1 Kings 8:22–36, 41–51

UNIT TWO. THE BROKEN KINGDOM (1 KINGS 12—16)

Lesson 3	A Leader's Foolish Choice	1 Kings 12:1–20
Lesson 4	So Bad So Soon	1 Kings 15:9–19; 16:29–33

UNIT THREE. PROPHETS AT WORK (1 KINGS 17—2 KINGS 8)

Lesson 5	A Call to Full Commitment	1 Kings 18:1–2, 17–39
Lesson 6	Time to Listen	1 Kings 19:1–18
Lesson 7	Speaking Truth to Power—Alone	1 Kings 22:6–28
Lesson 8	Extending God's Help to a "Foreigner"	2 Kings 5:1–19a

UNIT FOUR. MISSING THE LAST CHANCE (2 KINGS 9—17)

Lesson 9	Drifting Toward Disaster	2 Kings 14:23–29; 15:8–10, 13–14, 17–30
Lesson 10	Death of a Nation	2 Kings 17:1–18, 21–23

UNIT FIVE. MISSING THE LAST CHANCE: THE SEQUEL (2 KINGS 18—25)

Lesson 11	When the Situation Is Desperate	2 Kings 18:1–19, 29–31; 19:1–11, 14–20
Lesson 12	The Only Hope	2 Kings 22:1—23:4
Lesson 13	The Bitter End	2 Kings 23:31–32, 36–37; 24:8–9, 18–20; 25:8–21

NOTES

1. Unless otherwise indicated, all Scripture quotations in this *Adult Bible Study Guide* on 1 and 2 Kings are from the New International Version.
2. An additional word on where 1 and 2 Kings fits: 1 and 2 Chronicles covers a good bit of the same ground as 1 and 2 Kings. Chronicles, though, comes at this period of time from a different perspective. Where Kings is concerned with why the destruction happened, Chronicles is more concerned with giving details from Judah's history that would aid in rebuilding the Jewish nation through defining who was a Jew and how true Jews were to live.
3. Listing a book does not imply full agreement by the writers or BAPTISTWAY with all of its comments.

The (Supposed) Glory Days

UNIT ONE

1 Kings 1–11

The title to this unit, "The (Supposed) Glory Days," is a reminder that things are not always what they seem at first glance. Successes and accomplishments of a leader, a people, or a nation can turn out to be tarnished and insubstantial on closer examination.

This first unit in Kings begins with David and who would succeed him as king, which turned out to be Solomon. The unit largely deals with Solomon's exploits. The passage of Scripture included in this unit (1 Kings 1—11) pictures Solomon as a great leader and a pious leader, but also ultimately as a failed leader. The Bible's judgment on Solomon, this exceedingly wise king who built the temple, was that "his heart had turned away from the Lord, the God of Israel, who had appeared to him twice" (1 Kings 11:9).

The lessons in this unit focus on Solomon's good points and on what would have been considered Israel's "glory days." In secular terms, there was indeed much about Solomon's reign that would have made the description "glory days" appropriate. It is not to be forgotten, however, that the Bible does not consider Solomon's glory days to be completely glorious. Solomon's failures were lurking in the background and eventually overwhelmed him.[1]

UNIT ONE. 1 KINGS 1—11 THE (SUPPOSED) GLORY DAYS (1 KINGS 1—11)

Lesson 1	The Right Place to Begin	1 Kings 2:10–12; 3:1–15
Lesson 2	Prayer to a God Who Keeps Promises	1 Kings 8:22–36, 41–51

NOTES

1. Unless otherwise indicated, all Scripture quotations in unit 1 are from the New International Version.

Focal Text
1 Kings 2:10–12; 3:1–15

Background
1 Kings 1—3

Main Idea
Seeking God's wisdom is the right beginning place for any leader.

Question to Explore
Where does good leadership begin?

Study Aim
To evaluate Solomon's prayer and God's response and identify implications for leadership

Study and Action Emphases
- Affirm the Bible as our authoritative guide for life and ministry
- Develop a growing, vibrant faith
- Equip people for servant leadership

LESSON ONE: The Right Place to Begin

Quick Read
Learning the difference between knowledge and wisdom is an important key to good leadership.

1 AND 2 KINGS: *Leaders and Followers—Failed and Faithful*

I once asked a group of church folk, "What would you do if you suddenly received a million dollars?" One answered, "First, I would give a tithe to the church." Others in the circle stated a desire to help the church, reduce world hunger, provide clothing for orphans, and so forth. All of these are noble and honorable ideas. However, when my turn came, I said, "I would put it all on my credit card bill as far as it would go." I was implying, of course, that not even a million dollars would actually cover my debt!

Now, I realize that some who read this lesson might be quick to criticize my less than "holy" answer. However, the statement quickly drew laughter and reminded the group that most of us are not nearly so noble in real life with less money, fame, power or talents. We often use such gifts from God in selfish ways.

After David had died and Solomon had been installed on the throne as Israel's third king, God gave the new ruler a choice of anything his heart would desire. The story of God's remarkable offer and Solomon's unselfish request is the subject of this Bible study. Solomon began his reign by choosing wisdom instead of wealth or power. While some of his later choices provided a poor example for his successors, he began his reign in the right way.

1 Kings 2:10–12

¹⁰Then David rested with his fathers and was buried in the City of David. ¹¹He had reigned forty years over Israel—seven years in Hebron and thirty-three in Jerusalem. ¹²So Solomon sat on the throne of his father David, and his rule was firmly established.

1 Kings 3:1–15

¹Solomon made an alliance with Pharaoh king of Egypt and married his daughter. He brought her to the City of David until he finished building his palace and the temple of the LORD, and the wall around Jerusalem. ²The people, however, were still sacrificing at the high places, because a temple had not yet been built for the Name of the LORD. ³Solomon showed his love for the LORD by walking according to the statutes of his father David, except that he offered sacrifices and burned incense on the high places. ⁴The king went to Gibeon to offer sacrifices, for that was the most important high place, and Solomon offered a thousand burnt offerings on that altar. ⁵At Gibeon the LORD appeared to Solomon during

> the night in a dream, and God said, "Ask for whatever you want me to give you." ⁶Solomon answered, "You have shown great kindness to your servant, my father David, because he was faithful to you and righteous and upright in heart. You have continued this great kindness to him and have given him a son to sit on his throne this very day.
>
> ⁷"Now, O Lord my God, you have made your servant king in place of my father David. But I am only a little child and do not know how to carry out my duties. ⁸Your servant is here among the people you have chosen, a great people, too numerous to count or number. ⁹So give your servant a discerning heart to govern your people and to distinguish between right and wrong. For who is able to govern this great people of yours?" ¹⁰The Lord was pleased that Solomon had asked for this. ¹¹So God said to him, "Since you have asked for this and not for long life or wealth for yourself, nor have asked for the death of your enemies but for discernment in administering justice, ¹²I will do what you have asked. I will give you a wise and discerning heart, so that there will never have been anyone like you, nor will there ever be. ¹³Moreover, I will give you what you have not asked for—both riches and honor—so that in your lifetime you will have no equal among kings. ¹⁴And if you walk in my ways and obey my statutes and commands as David your father did, I will give you a long life." ¹⁵Then Solomon awoke—and he realized it had been a dream. He returned to Jerusalem, stood before the ark of the Lord's covenant and sacrificed burnt offerings and fellowship offerings. Then he gave a feast for all his court.

The Death of David (2:10–12)

David's death created a time of crisis. The transition to Solomon as the next king was not smooth or easy. The handsome Adonijah, David's oldest son, wanted to be Israel's next king. First Kings 1—2 relates the intrigue that surrounded the approaching death of the old king.

David was on his deathbed when Adonijah made his move (1 Kings 1:5–10). Adonijah knew David's death was imminent. He garnered horses and chariots, fifty men, the support of David's old general Joab, and Abiathar the priest. Adonijah offered a large sacrifice of sheep and cattle to inaugurate his ascension to the throne. Next, he prepared a celebration by inviting all his brothers—David's other sons—and the royal officials of Judah to a feast. Solomon, the prophet Nathan, the priest Benaiah, and the royal guard were not invited.

Bathsheba, Solomon's mother, appealed to David to fulfill his promise that Solomon would be the next king of Israel (1:11–17). Through a series of events that David ordered, Solomon was declared the king of Israel. Solomon assumed the throne and became the true and legitimate king of Israel (1:28–53). Adonijah, Joab, and Abiathar quickly professed their allegiance to Solomon.

> "What would you do if you suddenly received a million dollars?"

David, in the last few days of his life, sent for Solomon. The old king offered his son advice about being ruler over Israel. He cautioned Solomon, "'I am about to go the way of all the earth,' he said. 'So be strong, show yourself a man, and observe what the LORD your God requires: Walk in his ways, and keep his decrees and commands, his laws and requirements, as written in the Law of Moses, so that you may prosper in all you do and wherever you go'" (2:2–3).

In addition to this sage advice, David instructed Solomon on how to settle matters against Joab and Shemei, who had cursed David. Joab had assassinated Abner, King Saul's general, while David was concluding a peace treaty with Saul's army (2 Samuel 3:26–27). Joab also assassinated Amasa, his cousin and second in command, for failing to act quickly during the rebellion of Sheba, the Benjaminite (2 Sam. 20:10).

Solomon

Solomon began his reign around 961 B.C. The prophet Nathan had given him the name Jedidiah (*loved by the Lord*) at his birth (2 Sam. 12:25). "Solomon" means *peaceful*, which describes his forty-year reign with no major wars or conflicts. He was a master builder—building a palace, God's temple, and many buildings and fortifications throughout Israel's borders. Solomon also expanded the borders of Israel to their greatest reach through peace treaty marriages. Under Solomon, Israel gained international importance in the Middle East. He had great wealth and a large army.

Solomon's greatest mistakes were his marriages to 700 wives and 300 concubines (1 Kings 11:3–4). Unfortunately, too, Solomon pressed Israelites into slave labor to accomplish his many building programs. Likewise, he increased taxes.

Such acts made Solomon unpopular in his latter days. Solomon's unpopularity set the stage for the rebellion that took place at his death and for the subsequent split between the ten northern tribes, called Israel, and the two southern tribes, called Judah. He also built "high places" for the worship of foreign gods.

Shemei's treachery occurred while David was fleeing his rebellious son, Absalom. Shemei approached David and his army. Scurrying along the hillside as David and his troops passed, Shemei began cursing David and pelting him with dirt and pebbles. Shemei said, "Get out, get out, you man of blood, you scoundrel! The LORD has repaid you for all the blood you shed in the household of Saul, in whose place you have reigned. The LORD has handed the kingdom over to your son Absalom. You have come to ruin because you are a man of blood!" (2 Sam. 16:7–8). David prevented his troops from taking any action against Shemei. Instead, David pledged not to kill him (2 Sam. 19:23). However, on his deathbed, David placed Shemei's fate in the hands of Solomon, calling on Solomon to put Shemei to death.

Solomon carried out his father's wishes concerning both Joab and Shemei. Furthermore, he had Adonijah killed as he solidified his claim to the throne (1 Kings 2:13–25).

Solomon's Imperfections (3:1–3)

Although Solomon loved the Lord "by walking according to the statutes of his father David" (1 Kings 3:3), he was not perfect. Like all of us, Solomon sometimes chose expediency rather than obedience to God.

At the beginning of his reign, Solomon made a peace treaty with Egypt and sealed it by marrying the Pharaoh's daughter. In doing so, Solomon ignored the standards of God's covenant with Israel. God specifically instructed Israel's kings not to take many wives or accumulate large amounts of silver and gold (Deuteronomy 17:17). Joshua delivered a similar warning in his farewell address to Israel (Joshua 23:12–13).

> *Christian leadership originates from a servant's heart.*

God's prohibition against marrying foreigners was not a law against interracial marriage, as some have understood it. Instead, it was a prohibition against marriage to unbelievers. God knew such marriages would introduce pagan religions into Israel's culture. Solomon's many wives and concubines certainly fulfilled those fears. Paul echoed God's warning about not marrying a non-believer in 1 Corinthians 6:14.

A second fault of Solomon was that he offered sacrifices to pagan gods in the "high places." (See sidebar on "High Places.") "On a hill east of

Jerusalem, Solomon built a high place for Chemosh the detestable god of Moab, and for Molech the detestable god of the Ammonites. He did the same for all his foreign wives, who burned incense and offered sacrifices to their gods" (1 Kings 11:7–8). For this, Solomon fell out of favor with God. Rather than Solomon leading his wives to a commitment to Yahweh, the pagan wives led Solomon to split his commitment between God and their pagan gods.

> *One can have much knowledge but no wisdom.*

Solomon's Wise Beginning (3:4–15)

Solomon traveled to Gibeon where he offered a thousand burnt offerings to God. In 1 Kings 3:4, the term "high place" was not a place of pagan worship. The text makes clear that this "high place" was dedicated solely to the worship of Yahweh. God obviously was pleased with the young king and his offering.

Consequently, God made the unbelievable offer to Solomon, "Ask for whatever you want me to give you" (3:5). What would any of us do with such an offer from God? How might we reply?

Solomon began his answer with gratitude for the many kindnesses God had bestowed on his father David and continued to bestow on him. He believed God's kindnesses were a response to David's devotion to God. God does bless obedience. Such blessings are not always material but sometimes are spiritual in nature. God blesses every faithfully obedient person with everlasting life—not because of a person's work, but rather because of one's faith.

Note how Solomon used the term "servant" in verse 7. Although he was a king of people, he was also a servant of God. Solomon wisely saw that true godly work begins in servanthood to God's will. No Christian leader is a good leader if he or she does not understand this great truth. We do not lead by our own wisdom and knowledge. Christian leadership

> *Good leaders do not demand allegiance.*

originates from a servant's heart. We must beware of those who command that we follow them because they are educated or knowledgeable. One can have much knowledge but no wisdom.

"High Places"

This term in Scripture usually refers to pagan places of worship. Such altars or shrines were built on high ground to be nearer the alleged deity during worship. The author of 1 and 2 Kings (and other Old Testament writers) repeatedly condemned these places of pagan worship. Throughout the Scriptures, pagans would sacrifice children; perform lewd sexual rituals; and dance, eat, and drink to excess in the high places as forms of pagan worship.

Verses 8–9 demonstrate one of Solomon's finest moments. This humble request—not for fame, long life, power, or great riches—was the basis of God's decision to bless Solomon not only with a discerning heart but also with all the things he did not request. Solomon was catapulted into fame, long life, great riches, and power because of his humility.

A wise Christian leader is humble. Good leaders do not *demand* allegiance. Good leaders *earn* leadership through being trustworthy, demonstrating wisdom, and being humble. All church leaders should heed Solomon's example.

Solomon returned to Jerusalem and offered sacrifices before the ark of the covenant. These are called "burnt offerings and fellowship offerings" in our Scripture text. The "burnt offerings" were probably a continuation of the sacrifices he made at Gibeon, but the "peace offerings" are offerings of thanksgiving. Solomon showed his deep devotion and gratitude to God for giving him wisdom and the other gifts.

> *Good leaders earn leadership through being trustworthy, demonstrating wisdom, and being humble.*

Evidence of Solomon's Wisdom (3:16–28)

The story of the two prostitutes' dispute over the parenthood of a baby boy illustrates that God did, indeed, give Solomon the ability to discern between what was good and what was evil. Both women lived together and had babies born within three days of one another. Unfortunately, one woman went to sleep with her baby near her and during her sleep apparently rolled over on the baby, smothering it. When she awoke and realized what had happened, she swapped her dead baby for the other prostitute's baby boy. When the second woman awoke, she realized the treachery of

1 AND 2 KINGS: *Leaders and Followers—Failed and Faithful*

the first woman. However, since others could not tell which of the two was lying, the dispute came before King Solomon.

After both women claimed ownership of the living child, Solomon declared it was impossible to tell which woman was lying. Therefore, he asked for a sword and declared he would divide the child into two pieces so that each woman could have half of the living boy.

> *Although Solomon was far from perfect, his prayer requesting God's wisdom provides a model for leadership today.*

Horror struck the true mother. Realizing it would be better for her son to live rather then die she pleaded with Solomon not to do such a thing. Instead, she said to give the living baby to the other woman. The false mother revealed her evil lie by agreeing that neither woman should have the child. She encouraged the king to cut the boy in half so that neither would have a son. Solomon awarded the child to the true mother.

Solomon's wise action illustrated that God had indeed given him a "wise and discerning heart" (3:10) in response to his humble request (3:9). Although Solomon was far from perfect, his prayer requesting God's wisdom provides a model for leadership today.

QUESTIONS

1. What qualities should a Christian leader exhibit? In your opinion, do we expect perfection in our Christian leaders? Should we?

2. Should a Christian marry an unbeliever? How should a person who becomes a Christian act toward an unbelieving spouse?

3. What qualities did Solomon have that we should try to apply to our lives? What qualities did he have that we should avoid?

4. How would you respond if God said to you, "Ask for whatever you want me to give you"?

Focal Text
1 Kings 8:22–36, 41–51

Background
1 Kings 7:1—9:9

Main Idea
God calls for faithfulness to him as we pray for our needs to be met.

Question to Explore
Is authentic prayer a mark of strength or weakness, particularly on the part of leaders?

Study Aim
To evaluate my prayers in light of the main emphases of Solomon's prayer and determine how I may need to change the way I pray

Study and Action Emphases
- Affirm the Bible as our authoritative guide for life and ministry
- Share the gospel with all people
- Develop a growing, vibrant faith
- Value all people as created in the image of God
- Equip people for servant leadership

LESSON TWO

Prayer to a God Who Keeps Promises

Quick Read
To be an effective Christian, one must maintain a vibrant prayer life with God. We must realize that God wants to speak with us.

1 AND 2 KINGS: *Leaders and Followers—Failed and Faithful*

Prayer matters! Prayer is one of our most important tools for effective Christian living. Prayer is how we stay in direct communication with God.

God enjoys communicating with humanity. We see that delight as God speaks to us through Scripture, through his prophets and apostles, and through his Son, Jesus Christ. God also enjoys our response to his efforts to speak to us. We respond to God through prayer, worship, Bible reading, study, music, and obedience to his will.

Prayer is a wonderful privilege from God. Since Jesus acts as our high priest, we have direct access to God. We need no priest, minister, or other go-between. We believe that the God of the universe actually hears our individual prayers. I find it wonderful that a majestic and glorious God is interested in our human thoughts and words that are directed to him.

Many of us know of people who have the ability to speak beautifully to God. The renowned preacher Peter Marshall (1902—1949) was a man of prayer. He emigrated from Scotland to the United States in 1927. Although he arrived penniless, he soon made his way into the Presbyterian ministry. He served as Chaplain of the United States Senate from 1947 to 1949. Government workers would leave their jobs and crowd into the Senate gallery to hear him when he prayed. His prayers were moving, thoughtful, sincere, honest, and extremely personal. Some of his prayers were only one or two sentences long. He almost never offered prayers more than two minutes in length. Yet, workers made time in their day to hear Peter Marshall pray.

Why? The answer is simple. Peter Marshall prayed as if he was actually talking to God. He shut out all of life's distractions and offered prayer from deep within his soul.[1]

Meaningful prayers abound in the Bible. In this Bible lesson, we will explore Solomon's great prayer asking God to bless the new temple. I consider this to be one of the greatest prayers in the Bible. Solomon showed his sincerity and humbleness in the requests he uttered to God. We need to adopt this kind of sincerity and humility in our prayer lives.

1 Kings 8:22–36, 41–51

[22] Then Solomon stood before the altar of the LORD in front of the whole assembly of Israel, spread out his hands toward heaven [23] and said: "O LORD, God of Israel, there is no God like you in heaven above

or on earth below—you who keep your covenant of love with your servants who continue wholeheartedly in your way. **24**You have kept your promise to your servant David my father; with your mouth you have promised and with your hand you have fulfilled it—as it is today.

25 "Now LORD, God of Israel, keep for your servant David my father the promises you made to him when you said, 'You shall never fail to have a man to sit before me on the throne of Israel, if only your sons are careful in all they do to walk before me as you have done.' **26** And now, O God of Israel, let your word that you promised your servant David my father come true.

27 "But will God really dwell on earth? The heavens, even the highest heaven, cannot contain you. How much less this temple I have built! **28** Yet give attention to your servant's prayer and his plea for mercy, O LORD my God. Hear the cry and the prayer that your servant is praying in your presence this day. **29** May your eyes be open toward this temple night and day, this place of which you said, 'My Name shall be there,' so that you will hear the prayer your servant prays toward this place. **30** Hear the supplication of your servant and of your people Israel when they pray toward this place. Hear from heaven, your dwelling place, and when you hear, forgive.

31 "When a man wrongs his neighbor and is required to take an oath and he comes and swears the oath before your altar in this temple, **32** then hear from heaven and act. Judge between your servants, condemning the guilty and bringing down on his own head what he has done. Declare the innocent not guilty, and so establish his innocence.

33 "When your people Israel have been defeated by an enemy because they have sinned against you, and when they turn back to you and confess your name, praying and making supplication to you in this temple, **34** then hear from heaven and forgive the sin of your people Israel and bring them back to the land you gave to their fathers.

35 "When the heavens are shut up and there is no rain because your people have sinned against you, and when they pray toward this place and confess your name and turn from their sin because you have afflicted them, **36** then hear from heaven and forgive the sin of your servants, your people Israel. Teach them the right way to live, and send rain on the land you gave your people for an inheritance.

. . . .

41 "As for the foreigner who does not belong to your people Israel but has come from a distant land because of your name— **42** for men will hear of your great name and your mighty hand and your outstretched arm—when he comes and prays toward this temple, ⁴³then hear from heaven, your dwelling place, and do whatever the foreigner asks of you, so that all the peoples of the earth may know your name and fear you, as do your own people Israel, and may know that this house I have built bears your Name.

⁴⁴"When your people go to war against their enemies, wherever you send them, and when they pray to the Lord toward the city you have chosen and the temple I have built for your Name, ⁴⁵then hear from heaven their prayer and their plea, and uphold their cause.

⁴⁶"When they sin against you—for there is no one who does not sin—and you become angry with them and give them over to the enemy, who takes them captive to his own land, far away or near; ⁴⁷and if they have a change of heart in the land where they are held captive, and repent and plead with you in the land of their conquerors and say, 'We have sinned, we have done wrong, we have acted wickedly'; ⁴⁸and if they turn back to you with all their heart and soul in the land of their enemies who took them captive, and pray to you toward the land you gave their fathers, toward the city you have chosen and the temple I have built for your Name; ⁴⁹then from heaven, your dwelling place, hear their prayer and their plea, and uphold their cause. ⁵⁰And forgive your people, who have sinned against you; forgive all the offenses they have committed against you, and cause their conquerors to show them mercy; ⁵¹for they are your people and your inheritance, whom you brought out of Egypt, out of that iron-smelting furnace.

Building the Temple of God (1 Kings 5–7)

The story of Solomon's prayer begins with the building of the Jerusalem temple. David had started the project by gathering materials. In 1 Chronicles 22:14, he said to Solomon, "I have taken great pains to provide for the temple of the Lord a hundred thousand talents of gold, a million talents of silver, quantities of bronze and iron too great to be weighed, and wood and stone. And you may add to them." According to notes in the New International Version on this verse, a hundred thousand talents of gold is 3,750 tons, and a million talents of silver is 37,500 tons.

Solomon began the project in the fourth year of his reign. When Hiram, King of Tyre, heard that Solomon was ready to build the temple, he offered timber and workers to transport cedar logs down to Jerusalem

(1 Kings 5:1–12). Using conscripted labor, Solomon sent thirty thousand men to cut timber, eighty thousand stonecutters, seventy thousand carriers, and thirty three hundred supervisors (5:13–16). Solomon did not force any Israelites into slavery to accomplish the building. Instead, he used the non-Hebrews who lived in the land (9:20–22a).

First Kings 6:1–10 describes the dimensions of the structure. Solomon spared no expense. The beauty of the decorated interior and furniture is described in 1 Kings 6:14–36. You would do well to read this passage to review the beautiful design and use of precious metals in the building. First Kings 7:14–50 describes the magnificence of the outside of the temple, along with its many outdoor utensils. Workers took seven years to build the temple (6:38).

Prayer matters!

The Ark Moved to the New Temple (8:1–21)

Moving the ark of the covenant from the tabernacle in southern Jerusalem (the City of David) into the new temple was a momentous occasion. The grand procession included all the priests and the Levites, the elders of the twelve tribes, King Solomon, and an assemblage of Israelites. They carried

Other Hebrew Temples and Shrines

The Hebrew Old Testament had two words translated "temple": (1) *bayit*—house (of God); and (2) *hikhal*—palace (of Yahweh). Both Hebrew words refer to a holy place rather than a structure.

The Bible indicates the existence of several Israelite temples in addition to the one finally built in Jerusalem. All of these were more than just a "high place" or an altar located outside. The tabernacle was God's meeting place with Moses, and subsequently, with the priests of Israel. The Scriptures mention other temples or shrines at Shiloh (Joshua 19:51), Gilgal (1 Samuel 10:8), Mizpah (1 Sam. 7:6), Nob (1 Sam. 21:1), and Ephraim (Judges 17:8). It does not appear that any of these sites continued to function for any length of time after Solomon's temple.

The illegitimate temples erected by the Northern kingdom at Dan and Bethel were never recognized by all Hebrews (or God) as valid houses for the worship of Yahweh.

1 and 2 Kings: *Leaders and Followers—Failed and Faithful*

The Jerusalem Temple

Solomon completed the Jerusalem temple about 954 B.C. The Babylonians destroyed it in 587–586 B.C. Zerubbabel's temple was a new temple built on the location of Solomon's temple. It was completed about 515 B.C. (See Ezra 1:1–4 and 6:14–16.) Although the Roman general Pompey captured this temple in 63 B.C., he did not destroy it. Herod the Great decided to make the temple bigger and better to please the Jews. The work was begun sometime during his reign from 37—4 B.C., but this temple was not completed until about A.D. 60. Titus destroyed it in A.D. 70 in order to crush the Jewish revolt.

the ark, the tabernacle, and all the furniture and implements of the tabernacle to the new house of God. Solomon sacrificed so many sheep and cattle that their number could not be accurately recorded (8:5).

As soon as the priests placed the ark in its proper place, they withdrew. Immediately, a "cloud filled the temple of the LORD. And the priests could not perform their service because of the cloud, for the glory of the LORD filled his temple" (8:10b–11). Solomon declared that the cloud was a manifestation of God's presence taking up residence in the new temple.

We do not leave God behind at the church building when we exit on Sunday.

Solomon acknowledged his father's desire to build a house for God (8:17–19). Through Nathan the prophet, God had told David that he was not the one who would build a house for God (2 Samuel 7:5–17). Instead, God had promised to establish David's house forever: "When your days are over and you rest with your fathers, I will raise up your offspring to succeed you, who will come from your own body, and I will establish his kingdom" (2 Sam. 7:12). Along with many Bible interpreters, I consider this prophecy to refer ultimately to Jesus.

Solomon Dedicates the Temple (8:22–30)

Note that Solomon stood while praying before God. Later in this same prayer, he knelt (1 Kings 8:54). More important than one's literal posture is the attitude of one's soul. Solomon was engrossed in his prayer, and his soul dictated his posture. Whatever posture we assume in prayer, it should be respectful.

Solomon addressed God's greatness in his prayer. He stated that there is no God like Yahweh. The king thanked God for keeping his promises to David. He called on God to fulfill the promise of keeping a son of David on Israel's throne. This son would always have access to God. David and Solomon would not have understood this promise in Messianic terms, but later generations of faithful believers longed for God to send a Messiah, who would fulfill this promise. In first-century Judaism, this verse was considered a messianic promise.

In 1 Kings 8:27, Solomon acknowledged that no dwelling made by human beings could ever be large or grand enough to contain God. We would do well to remember these wise words. God does not live in a cathedral or any place built by humans. We do not leave God behind at the church building when we exit on Sunday. God is not limited by time and space. God visits us in the places of our daily lives as well as in our houses of worship.

God visits us in the places of our daily lives as well as in our houses of worship.

Solomon's Prayer on Behalf of Israel (8:31–51)

Solomon outlined in these verses the many reasons one would come to the temple. The seven petitions in this prayer are the kind one might utter in God's temple. Obviously, Solomon never intended that this would be an exhaustive list of prayers permitted at the temple. All of the petitions seek God's forgiveness (8:30).

The first petition (8:31–32) would occur when one had wronged a neighbor. "Wronged" translates the Hebrew word for *trespass*, meaning *crossing the boundary of a law*. Solomon recognized that God is the true judge in such matters. If a person would come to the temple to swear a matter to be true, God would judge the truthfulness of that oath. Even if people cannot tell who is telling the truth, God can and does.

The second petition (8:33–34) involves Israel's defeat in battle because of sin and the failure to confess it. In Leviticus 26:17 and Deuteronomy 28:25, God declared he would turn against Israel in battle if they failed to keep God's commands. If this happened, the people must come to the temple and pray with true repentance.

Not all natural disasters are God's punishment, but all natural disasters remind us how frail we are before God.

1 AND 2 KINGS: *Leaders and Followers—Failed and Faithful*

The third petition (8:35–36) would be needed when God sent drought on the land because of the people's sin. In Leviticus 26:19–20, God warned, "I will break down your stubborn pride and make the sky above you like iron and the ground beneath you like bronze. Your strength will be spent in vain, because your soil will not yield its crops, nor will the trees of the land yield their fruit." God can and does use nature as a method of punishment. We may dismiss too quickly the anger of God. Not all natural disasters are God's punishment, but all natural disasters remind us how frail we are before God.

> *If we wish to be effective Christians, we must develop sensitivity to our sinful actions and demonstrate a desire for correct behavior.*

The fourth petition (8:37–40) is similar to the previous reason for coming to God in repentance. Note that the list of natural disasters expands to include other types of agricultural plagues, diseases on people, and attacks on their cities by foreign invaders. Notice how personal this prayer is. Individuals pray. This is seen in the words, a "plea is made by any of your people Israel—each one aware of the afflictions of his own heart, and spreading out his hands toward this temple" (8:38). The prayer and repentance are personal. Solomon called on God to act on each person's prayer, according to the sincerity of his or her individual heart.

The fifth petition (8:41–43) takes a unique turn of thought. Solomon's prayer included Gentiles who might come to pray before God. The Hebrew temple had a "court of the Gentiles" as a place of prayer. You may recall that in the Gospels the temple priests had turned this outer court of prayer into a marketplace. Jesus was indignant that the Jews allowed such a corruption of purpose with no regard for Gentiles and God's desire to hear their prayers (Luke 19:45–46). Solomon asked God to hear and answer their prayers so that all the earth would hear about God and know how great God is.

> *Let us seek our gracious God in humble prayer, coupling prayer with living in faithfulness to God.*

The sixth petition (8:44–45) addresses the matter of going to war. War is always troubling. Throughout Christian history, Christians have struggled with involvement in war. This passage calls for the believer to bring the cause of war before God. It is necessary to be within the will of God in all such extreme matters. Prayer must precede war.

The final petition (8:46–51) involves each individual and his or her sins. Paul's words in Romans 3:23, "for all have sinned and fall short of the glory of God," find their roots here. When we sin, we are to appear before God and repent and ask forgiveness. Solomon asked God to forgive "all" (*every*) sin.

This great prayer outlines many occasions for prayer and repentance. First Kings 9:1–9 records the Lord's response to Solomon's prayer. Included in this response is a call for living "in integrity of heart and uprightness" (9:4).

If we wish to be effective Christians, we must develop sensitivity to our sinful actions and demonstrate a desire for correct behavior. Let us seek our gracious God in humble prayer, coupling prayer with living in faithfulness to God.

QUESTIONS

1. Honestly, how often do you pray?

2. Solomon listed seven reasons a person might offer prayer to God. Can you think of other reasons we might seek God in prayer?

3. In what ways does the average Christian try to confine God to temples, church buildings, and holy places?

NOTES

1. For more information, see Catherine Marshall, *A Man Called Peter* (Grand Rapids, MI: Chosen Books, 1951).

The Broken Kingdom

UNIT TWO

1 Kings 12–16

After Solomon, as God had warned, the united nation was broken into two unequal parts (see 1 Kings 11:12–13). The breach occurred when Rehoboam, Solomon's successor, made a foolish choice and was left with only one tribe to follow his leadership. Jeroboam, Rehoboam's rival who took the remaining tribes, did no better, though. In fact, he did worse. Jeroboam became known as the epitome of evil for leading Israel astray.

Beyond Rehoboam and Jeroboam, even the best (Asa of Judah, 15:9–24) of the leaders during this period was not very good and the worst (Ahab of Israel, 16:29–33) was about as bad as he could get. The question such poor leadership brings to mind is how this could have happened so soon after David in Israel's history.[1]

These lessons will lead us to consider the nature of true leadership from the standpoint of the disaster that occurs when leadership is poor. Lesson three focuses on Rehoboam's broken relationship with people who would have been his followers had he been a better leader. Lesson four uses bad examples of leadership to remind us of the positive direction in which good leaders must lead.

UNIT TWO. THE BROKEN KINGDOM (1 KINGS 12—16)

| Lesson 3 | A Leader's Foolish Choice | 1 Kings 12:1–20 |
| Lesson 4 | So Bad So Soon | 1 Kings 15:9–19; 16:29–33 |

NOTES

1. Unless otherwise indicated, all Scripture quotations in unit 2 are from the New International Version.

Focal Text
1 Kings 12:1–20

Background
1 Kings 11—12; 14:21–31

Main Idea
When a leader makes a foolish decision, the results can be tragic and longlasting.

Question to Explore
How can servants be leaders and leaders be servants?

Study Aim
To describe the foolish decision Rehoboam made and its implications for today

Study and Action Emphases
- Affirm the Bible as our authoritative guide for life and ministry
- Develop a growing, vibrant faith
- Equip people for servant leadership

LESSON THREE
A Leader's Foolish Choice

Quick Read
Rehoboam's foolish decision to increase the burden of taxes and labor on the people led the northern tribes to secede and select Jeroboam to be their king.

1 AND 2 KINGS: Leaders and Followers—Failed and Faithful

The future of Christianity depends on teaching the next generation to seek God. Parents must set good examples for their children through prayer and other actions that demonstrate true commitment to Christ. However, although we may be committed to Christ, our children may still turn away from God. This, of course, is very frightening. We hope that children will see our devotion to Christ and develop a firm commitment to him for themselves.

Parents, though, can make foolish choices. They may drift away from God and allow the desire for bigger houses, better cars, and boats and other recreational equipment to replace godly activities and serving Christ. They may work at jobs that require so much time that they have little left to nurture family and serve God.

Children whose parents make foolish choices may find their spiritual growth stunted. Children may embrace materialism, practice ungodly lifestyles, find themselves in shallow marriages, and exhibit a lack of commitment to God. They may attend worship when there is nothing else to do. They may know nothing of serving through the church. They may offer little or no financial support to the church and to missions. However, they still may seek out God and his church for weddings and funerals.

Sadly, we are only one generation away from paganism. Such was the case with Solomon and the kings who came after him. Solomon did not follow the ways of his father, David. In his later years, he worshiped other gods.

Today's lesson about Solomon's son, Rehoboam, illustrates how quickly a new generation can turn away from God. Rehoboam never sought God's help or advice as he ruled Israel.

1 Kings 12:1–20

¹Rehoboam went to Shechem, for all the Israelites had gone there to make him king. ²When Jeroboam son of Nebat heard this (he was still in Egypt, where he had fled from King Solomon), he returned from Egypt. ³So they sent for Jeroboam, and he and the whole assembly of Israel went to Rehoboam and said to him: ⁴"Your father put a heavy yoke on us, but now lighten the harsh labor and the heavy yoke he put on us, and we will serve you."

⁵Rehoboam answered, "Go away for three days and then come back to me." So the people went away.

⁶Then King Rehoboam consulted the elders who had served his father Solomon during his lifetime. "How would you advise me to answer these people?" he asked.

⁷They replied, "If today you will be a servant to these people and serve them and give them a favorable answer, they will always be your servants."

⁸But Rehoboam rejected the advice the elders gave him and consulted the young men who had grown up with him and were serving him. ⁹He asked them, "What is your advice? How should we answer these people who say to me, 'Lighten the yoke your father put on us'?"

¹⁰The young men who had grown up with him replied, "Tell these people who have said to you, 'Your father put a heavy yoke on us, but make our yoke lighter'—tell them, 'My little finger is thicker than my father's waist. ¹¹My father laid on you a heavy yoke; I will make it even heavier. My father scourged you with whips; I will scourge you with scorpions.'"

¹²Three days later Jeroboam and all the people returned to Rehoboam, as the king had said, "Come back to me in three days." ¹³The king answered the people harshly. Rejecting the advice given him by the elders, ¹⁴he followed the advice of the young men and said, "My father made your yoke heavy; I will make it even heavier. My father scourged you with whips; I will scourge you with scorpions." ¹⁵So the king did not listen to the people, for this turn of events was from the LORD, to fulfill the word the LORD had spoken to Jeroboam son of Nebat through Ahijah the Shilonite.

¹⁶When all Israel saw that the king refused to listen to them, they answered the king:

"What share do we have in David,
 what part in Jesse's son?
To your tents, O Israel!
 Look after your own house, O David!"

So the Israelites went home. ¹⁷But as for the Israelites who were living in the towns of Judah, Rehoboam still ruled over them.

¹⁸King Rehoboam sent out Adoniram, who was in charge of forced labor, but all Israel stoned him to death. King Rehoboam, however, managed to get into his chariot and escape to Jerusalem. ¹⁹So Israel has been in rebellion against the house of David to this day.

²⁰When all the Israelites heard that Jeroboam had returned, they sent and called him to the assembly and made him king over all Israel. Only the tribe of Judah remained loyal to the house of David.

Solomon's Folly (11:1–43)

This chapter reveals some of King Solomon's weaknesses. We ask as we read this chapter, *How could such a wise and blest man become so foolish?* Solomon abandoned a firm commitment to God and mixed his devotion to God with that of other gods. As we learned in lesson one, God warned Israel's kings not to marry many wives or foreign wives (Exodus 34:15–16; Deuteronomy 17:17) because they would turn the king's heart away from God. This is precisely what happened to Solomon. He had 700 wives and 300 concubines from many pagan nations surrounding Israel. (What was he thinking?) By these so-called *treaty marriages,* Solomon established non-aggression agreements with surrounding nations.

> *Refusal to use our plentiful resources to alleviate the world's suffering is sinful.*

Not only did Solomon marry these foreign women, but he also built temples to their gods. Eventually, he himself became involved in the worship of pagan deities (1 Kings 11:4). God pronounced judgment on Solomon for his religious unfaithfulness and foretold that there would be two kingdoms instead of one united nation (11:13). The Northern kingdom (or Israel) would have ten tribes and the Southern kingdom (or Judah) would be composed of the two tribes of Judah and Benjamin.

Because of Solomon's foolishness, God also sent various adversaries to harass Solomon during his reign. Hadad the Edomite (11:14–22) and Rezon of Aram (11:23–25) were a nuisance to Solomon.

Solomon placed Jeroboam, an Ephraimite, in charge of the whole labor force of the house of Joseph (the tribes of Ephraim and Manasseh). Jeroboam became a man with great influence. Ahijah, a prophet from Shiloh (11:29), found Jeroboam and delivered God's message that God would give him the ten northern tribes of Israel so as to punish Solomon and his descendants for Solomon's unfaithfulness.

> *We are only one generation away from paganism.*

God cautioned Jeroboam to be faithful. If Jeroboam kept his allegiance to God alone, God would give him a name and dynasty like King David's (11:38).

Solomon tried to kill Jeroboam, but he escaped by fleeing to Egypt. When Solomon died, Jeroboam returned to challenge Solomon's son, Rehoboam, who had become king.

Rehoboam's Foolish Choice (12:1–20)

Solomon had abandoned total commitment to God to please his many wives and concubines. By doing so, Solomon created a climate of permissiveness in Israel. Rehoboam, his son, followed in his father's ungodly ways. Future kings and the people of Israel would also waver in their commitment to God. Expediency and selfishness became normal behavior.

Rehoboam's reign did not begin well and continued a downward spiral throughout his seventeen years in power. The first decision Rehoboam faced was whether to continue to tax Israel for expensive building projects and a lavish lifestyle for the court. The people of Israel wanted relief.

> *Good leaders do not forget the important principle that they are servants first.*

During the coronation at Shechem, Jeroboam, on behalf of the people, asked the king to lighten their burden and taxation (12:4). Jeroboam was a man of great influence. He pledged, on behalf of the Israelites outside of Judah, to become loyal subjects to Rehoboam, if Rehoboam would lighten the load. Rehoboam asked for three days to consider the request.

Rehoboam used the three days to seek advice on how to respond to the request. First, he sought the advice of the elders who had served Solomon. The elders knew that true leadership serves people and does not rule over

Solomon's Foreign Gods

First Kings 11:5–8 mentions three of the foreign gods Solomon worshiped—Ashtoreth (Asherah), a Canaanite fertility deity; Molech (Milcom), god of the Ammonites; and Chemosh, god of the Moabites. Other deities were also worshiped in Israel, but these are illustrations and not intended to be an exhaustive list.

Ashtoreth was the consort of El (or Baal). She was a fertility goddess. Her worship included sexual immorality and prostitution. The Ashtoreth pole was a sexual symbol, and Old Testament prophets frequently called for its destruction.

Molech (which means *king*) demanded human sacrifice. The sacrifice of babies and small children was common (2 Kings 23:10). Kings Ahaz (2 Kings 16:3) and Manasseh (2 Kings 21:6) sacrificed their children to this god.

The Bible mentions Chemosh, god of the Moabites, eight times, but we know very little about him or his worship. A Moabite king offered a child sacrifice to Chemosh in order to prevent Israel from destroying him (2 Kings 3:26).

them with an iron fist. Because of this principle and Jeroboam's influence, the elders advised Rehoboam to grant Jeroboam's request. (See small article, "Jeroboam, King of Israel.")

Rehoboam was not pleased with the elders' advice. Therefore, he sought the advice of younger men who had grown up with him. Like him, they were used to a lavish lifestyle (12:10–11). They enjoyed power and wealth. If Rehoboam were to lighten the taxes and stop the building projects, they would have fewer niceties. They offered self-centered, arrogant advice. They advised Rehoboam to *increase* the taxes and the workload. Rehoboam followed this foolish advice, which led to tragic results (12:16). The ten northern tribes no longer felt as though the house of David cared for their needs. They refused to continue to work for and serve Rehoboam. A rebellion occurred.

> Are the Christians of our generation living lives distinctly different from the unbelievers around us?

When Rehoboam sent his servant who was in charge of "forced labor" to the people, they stoned him to death and tried to stone Rehoboam (12:18). He barely escaped in his chariot. Immediately, the ten northern tribes made Jeroboam king over them. War between the Northern kingdom and the Southern kingdom continued through many generations until the Northern kingdom fell to the Assyrians in 722–721 B.C.. The Northern kingdom never came back into existence. Its people were scattered, and they lost their Jewish identity, heritage, and relationship to God.

Several lessons for us can be found in this disastrous story. We live in a wealthy and powerful society. Americans seldom appreciate the comfortable lifestyle we have in comparison to the many poor nations of the world. Refusal to use our plentiful resources to alleviate the world's suffering is sinful. Being a great nation with so much wealth and power is not wrong in itself. Not sharing our bounty with the less fortunate *is* wrong, however. Whereas America cannot solve all of the world's problems, we can help in matters of health, hunger, and clean water.

Furthermore, we learn another lesson here. Servanthood is essential to genuine leadership. Jesus was a servant and called on his followers to be servants of one another. He said, "Instead, whoever wants to become great among you must be your servant, and whoever wants to be first must be slave of all. For even the Son of Man did not come to be served, but to serve, and to give his life as a ransom for many" (Mark 10:43–44). Pastors, deacons, and other church leaders are not rulers of the church;

Jeroboam, King of Israel

Jeroboam was the first king of the Northern kingdom of Israel (around 928–907 B.C.). Because he feared his subjects would turn back to Judah, he built pagan shrines at Dan and Bethel and set up golden calves for the people to worship (12:25–33). God condemned Jeroboam, saying to him, "You have done more evil than all who lived before you. You have made for yourself other gods, idols made of metal" (13:9). Thus, God did not establish a dynasty for Jeroboam.

---

they are all servants. Good leaders do not forget the important principle that they are servants first. Rehoboam had forgotten this truth.

Like Father, Like Son (14:21–31)

Solomon provided an atmosphere of pagan worship in Israel. Rehoboam, his son, followed in his footsteps. Under Rehoboam, Judah did more evil in God's sight than any of their ancestors (1 Kings 14:22). Worship of Asherah occurred on "every high hill and under every spreading tree" (14:23). Although these statements ("every") are probably exaggerated for emphasis, the biblical author was pointing out that such places were numerous.

How we act speaks louder than how we believe.

According to verse 24, in addition to heterosexual immorality, the people practiced homosexual male prostitution. The people of Judah reverted to the paganism of the original inhabitants in Canaan. There was no difference between Judah and those former pagans. God was having little impact on their lives.

The lesson for our generation is obvious. Are the Christians of our generation living lives distinctly different from the unbelievers around us? Do our language, social habits, marriage commitments, use of money, use of time, and service to God's kingdom reflect our claims of being Christian?

God punished Rehoboam and Judah for their ungodliness. Shishak, king of Egypt, besieged Jerusalem in the fifth year of Rehoboam's reign. In Egypt, Shishak was called Sheshonk I (945–924 B.C.). He was from Libya and overthrew the weak pharaoh, thus founding the twenty-second dynasty. He was the pharaoh who gave asylum to Jeroboam when Jeroboam rebelled against Solomon (11:26).

1 AND 2 KINGS: *Leaders and Followers—Failed and Faithful*

When Shishak left Jerusalem, he took with him the treasures in the temple and in Rehoboam's palace. The author of Kings mentions that Shishak took the golden shields of David's "mighty warriors." These hung in the king's palace in Jerusalem. They were a testament—similar to military medals—to the bravery of many warriors who fought in David's army.

Rehoboam tried to cover his humiliation by Shishak by making bronze shields to replace the golden ones, but bronze is no substitute for gold. No amount of polishing would ever fool the people of Judah.

The last of Rehoboam's legacy states that he was continually at war with Jeroboam and the Northern kingdom (14:30). After seventeen years as king, Rehoboam died. He was remembered as a wicked king (15:3). If he had made different choices and followed God, his legacy would read differently.

We learn from Rehoboam that actions have lasting consequences. This lesson applies to every Christian. We can create an atmosphere of disobedience to God that will affect our children for future generations. If our children see us disregarding the teachings of God, they may be led to do the same thing in their lives. How we act speaks louder than how we believe. Words and actions must match. We cannot behave one way on Sunday during church and Bible study, and then behave in an opposite way in our homes, businesses, and neighborhoods.

> *Rehoboam serves as a negative example of behavior before God.*

Rehoboam serves as a negative example of behavior before God. We need to heed his mistakes. He refused to be a true servant-leader before God and to his people. He should have chosen to put his desires beneath the needs of his people. Because he did not, he lost a whole kingdom. Let us vow not to follow in the footsteps of Rehoboam.

Lesson 3: A Leader's Foolish Choice

QUESTIONS

1. In what ways can church leaders model Christian behavior for others?

2. What situations have you experienced that are similar to Rehoboam's wrong approach to leadership in this lesson?

3. What principles of good leadership can you identify from Rehoboam's wrong approach in this passage? What did he do right?

4. How important is age in being a good leader?

5. What practical steps might your church take to turn your community more toward obedience to God?

Focal Text
1 Kings 15:9–19; 16:29–33

Background
1 Kings 15:1—16:34

Main Idea
Where there is poor leadership, the people perish.

Question to Explore
How did things get so bad so soon in the history of God's people, and how can we keep it from happening to us?

Study Aim
To analyze the leadership of Asa and Ahab and identify implications for leadership today

Study and Action Emphases
- Affirm the Bible as our authoritative guide for life and ministry
- Develop a growing, vibrant faith
- Equip people for servant leadership

LESSON FOUR

So Bad So Soon

Quick Read
In order to change the sinful condition of our society, we need spiritual leaders who are willing to go against community standards, including the sinfulness of previous generations.

1 AND 2 KINGS: *Leaders and Followers—Failed and Faithful*

Clark Gable, in the 1939 Academy Award winning movie *Gone with the Wind*, shocked the American public of that day by uttering the most well-known of all curse words. Since then our society has become more accepting of even viler language in movies, books, magazines, and television.

In 1953, *Playboy Magazine* arrived at the local newsstands. Since then, a multitude of pornographic magazines and an explosion of pornography over the internet have infiltrated American culture. Although the revenues of the pornography industry are difficult to determine, Americans spent several billion dollars on pornography in 2003, perhaps as much as $8 billion to $10 billion.

When I was in high school, the drug of choice was alcohol. Today, it is still the most abused drug by high school students, but now alcohol abuse has become an issue for middle- and elementary-school-age children. In addition to alcohol, we see increased misuse of both illegal and prescription drugs. Drug use is epidemic in this country.

Furthermore, we live in a society where children are gunned down in schools and colleges. We see television reports of mass murders in shopping malls, in the workplace, and on the streets. Child molestation, spousal abuse, corporate greed, terror threats, and similar wrongs are common occurrences.

How did this happen? How did our society get so bad so soon? What caused all this sin and societal change? What could we have done differently? What can we do now? What role should the church have in improving the moral climate of our society?

These are important questions. Recognizing our sinful condition is not enough. We must do something to reverse the tide of growing evil in our communities. In addition to personal repentance, our society needs to turn back to the teachings of God found in the Scriptures. The leadership exhibited by the kings of Israel and Judah teaches us valuable lessons. Some of the kings were good; many were not. Godly leaders move us toward God while ungodly leaders allow us to stray.

Asa, King of Judah (15:9–24)

Asa (908–867 B.C.) was the fifth king of the Davidic dynasty. He was the grandson of Rehoboam and son of Abijah, who ruled only three years. Unfortunately, Abijah was evil like his father (1 Kings 15:3).

1 Kings 15:9–19

⁹In the twentieth year of Jeroboam king of Israel, Asa became king of Judah, ¹⁰and he reigned in Jerusalem forty-one years. His grandmother's name was Maacah daughter of Abishalom.

¹¹Asa did what was right in the eyes of the LORD, as his father David had done. ¹²He expelled the male shrine prostitutes from the land and got rid of all the idols his fathers had made. ¹³He even deposed his grandmother Maacah from her position as queen mother, because she had made a repulsive Asherah pole. Asa cut the pole down and burned it in the Kidron Valley. ¹⁴Although he did not remove the high places, Asa's heart was fully committed to the LORD all his life. ¹⁵He brought into the temple of the LORD the silver and gold and the articles that he and his father had dedicated.

¹⁶There was war between Asa and Baasha king of Israel throughout their reigns. ¹⁷Baasha king of Israel went up against Judah and fortified Ramah to prevent anyone from leaving or entering the territory of Asa king of Judah.

¹⁸Asa then took all the silver and gold that was left in the treasuries of the LORD's temple and of his own palace. He entrusted it to his officials and sent them to Ben-Hadad son of Tabrimmon, the son of Hezion, the king of Aram, who was ruling in Damascus. ¹⁹"Let there be a treaty between me and you," he said, "as there was between my father and your father. See, I am sending you a gift of silver and gold. Now break your treaty with Baasha king of Israel so he will withdraw from me."

1 Kings 16:29–33

²⁹In the thirty-eighth year of Asa king of Judah, Ahab son of Omri became king of Israel, and he reigned in Samaria over Israel twenty-two years. ³⁰Ahab son of Omri did more evil in the eyes of the LORD than any of those before him. ³¹He not only considered it trivial to commit the sins of Jeroboam son of Nebat, but he also married Jezebel daughter of Ethbaal king of the Sidonians, and began to serve Baal and worship him. ³²He set up an altar for Baal in the temple of Baal that he built in Samaria. ³³Ahab also made an Asherah pole and did more to provoke the LORD, the God of Israel, to anger than did all the kings of Israel before him.

Asa differed from the three kings who immediately preceded him. The Bible says he was a good king in God's sight (15:11). The author of Kings compares him favorably to his great-great-grandfather, David.

Even though Asa grew up in an environment of spiritual disobedience to God, he overcame this burden. Children do not have to continue in their parents' sins. Many children, then and now, have rejected the ungodliness of their parents. Asa was one such person. The Scriptures label eight of the nineteen kings of Judah "good kings." Only Hezekiah and Josiah receive higher praise in Scripture than Asa.

> *If we are to turn society back toward God, some children will need to reject the behavior of their parents.*

Although Asa was not perfect or sinless, as we shall soon see, he was a leader who set out to right the wrongful behavior of his royal predecessors and of the people of Judah. He ruled forty-one years in the Southern kingdom. At the beginning of his reign, he had peace in the land for ten years (2 Chronicles 14:1). During this time Asa instituted his religious reforms.

Asa stopped male prostitution (1 Kings 15:12), tore down altars to foreign deities, cut down Asherah poles, and commanded the people to keep the law (2 Chron. 14:2–5). His reforms included ridding the nation of the pagan worship promoted by his mother, Maacah—a daughter of Absalom, David's son. He removed her from the office of queen mother for her role in worshiping Asherah (1 Kings 15:13). He destroyed Asherah's image and the Asherah pole that his mother had made. God showed favor on Asa for taking these drastic steps of reform.

Baal Worship

"Baal" is a Semitic word for the Canaanite deity who was the god of fertility and weather. "Baal" means *owner, husband, lord,* or *master*. Baal was the son of Dagon, the Philistine god. Baal proved to be the most serious temptation the Israelites faced in the Promised Land. Throughout Israel's history, from the period of the judges until the Babylonian captivity, worship of Baal resulted in religious unfaithfulness to the true God, Yahweh.

Baal's consort was Asherah, the goddess of fertility. Together, they promoted sexual promiscuity in humans and agricultural growth in crops and animals.

In Scripture, Baal is often compounded with words to distinguish his activities. Baal-Berith *(lord of the covenant)*, Baal-Peor (a Moabite deity), Baal-Hamon *(lord of graciousness)*, and Baal-Judah *(lord of Judah)* are just some of the names found in Scripture. Perhaps the most famous compound name for Baal is Baal-Zebub *(lord of the flies)*. Baal-Zebub first occurs in 2 Kings 1:2 as a Philistine god.

How many of us are strong enough to take such steps? Asa went against the community standards and against his own mother in order to return Judah to reliance upon God. If we are to turn society back toward God, some children will need to reject the behavior of their parents.

> *How did our society get so bad so soon?*

Not all of Asa's works were good and noble. He failed to remove all of the "high places" of foreign deities. Some pagan worship continued without interruption. Asa's reforms did not go far enough. Yet, even with this failing, Asa was a man whose "heart was fully committed to the LORD all his life" (15:14).

Peace in Asa's reign did not last long. Baasha, king of Israel (906–883 B.C.), was the chronic enemy of Asa. Baasha openly attacked Judah (see 2 Chron. 16:1). Asa again acted unfaithfully. Instead of relying on God, he made a treaty with Ben-Hadad, the king of Aram and Damascus. Therefore, God sent the prophet Hanani to rebuke Asa for this failure (see 2 Chron. 16:7–10).

Asa stripped much of the gold and silver from the temple and from his palace to send to Ben-Hadad. With this gift, Asa asked Ben-Hadad to break his treaty with Baasha, which he did (1 Kings 15:20). Ben-Hadad then sent his army against the cities in Israel, forcing Baasha to retreat from Ramah to defend these cities. Then, Asa sent his men to get the unused fortifications at Ramah to fortify the city of Geba of Benjamin near Mizpah (15:22).

> *What role should the church have in improving the moral climate of our society?*

Asa's reforms continued beyond his lifetime. He had a positive spiritual influence on the life of his son, Jehoshaphat, who ruled Judah for twenty-five years (936–911 B.C.). Jehoshaphat followed in his father's footsteps and did right in God's eyes (22:41–43).

A Series of Evil Kings in Israel (15:25—16:28)

Although the kings of the Southern kingdom were far from perfect, the focus of these verses is on the evil the kings of Israel did. A succession of evil kings followed Israel's first king, Jeroboam. Nadab, the son of Jeroboam, ruled only two years before Baasha assassinated him. Baasha killed all of Jeroboam's descendants, wiping out his name in Israel as God had predicted through the prophet from Shiloh, Ahijah (14:10–11).

Baasha sinned in the same way Jeroboam had sinned. He did not walk in God's ways after God put him in power (16:2). He ruled seventeen years in Israel. When he died, his son, Elah, became king. Elah ruled for two years before he died at the hands of Zimri (16:9–10). Zimri, commander of half of the chariots in Israel's army, assassinated Elah and killed all the descendants of Baasha. Oddly, Zimri (around 882 B.C.) ruled as king of Israel for only one week.

When Israel's main body of troops heard that Zimri had killed King Elah, they made Omri, commander of Israel's army, king over Israel. Omri (882–871 B.C.) marched on Zimri at Tirzah. When Zimri saw that the battle for Tirzah was lost, he went into the king's house and set it on fire, taking his own life in the process (16:17–18).

How long will God be patient with our refusal to turn back to him?

Tibni challenged Omri's rule. The people were evenly divided in their support of the two claimants to the Israel's throne. Eventually, Tibni lost the battle and Omri's troops prevailed, killing him (16:21–22).

Omri ruled Israel from two locations. He ruled for the first six years from Tirzah. Later he built a palace at Samaria, which became Israel's permanent capital. Omri was even more evil than his forefathers. With each Israelite king, a downward spiral away from God continued.

Ahab, King of Israel (16:29–34)

Israel continued its downward plunge under Ahab (874–853 B.C.). Although the Bible soundly condemns Ahab, he was a very powerful king on the world's stage. His power and influence extended beyond Israel's borders.

Ramah

The exact location of Ramah (1 Kings 15:17) is uncertain. However, the Ramah mentioned in today's lesson is usually placed five miles north of Jerusalem on the border between Israel and Judah. This is near the town of Bethel and is probably the location where Deborah judged Israel in the twelfth century B.C. This same location was where the Assyrians camped on their way to destroy Judah (Isaiah 10:29).

Ahab continued to allow pagan worship and eventually joined his infamous wife Jezebel in worshiping Baal. He also set up an Asherah pole.

This kind of wicked leadership contributed to God's destruction of the Northern kingdom by the Assyrians in 722–721 B.C. God appealed to Israel on numerous occasions to repent. However, God's patience is not endless. When people refuse God's call to repentance, God sends judgment.

Is our society like ancient Israel's? We are plunging deeper into the pit of sinfulness. Our sins no longer embarrass us. We accept wickedness as part and parcel of daily affairs. We continue to ignore God's word. How long will God be patient with our refusal to turn back to him?

> *We Christians can make a difference both personally and collectively.*

We Christians can make a difference both personally and collectively. Personally, we can repent from our own sins. We can walk in a new direction under the leadership of the Holy Spirit and Scripture. Collectively, we can repent for our silence in the face of society's growing acceptance of sin. Our churches must become lighthouses in an increasingly dark society. We should shed light on the growing evil around us. Our churches need to stand up for the righteousness found in Scripture.

> *We need to return to God and make him our only God.*

It will take courage and resolve to fight against the tide of acceptance of sin. Good leadership must come from committed pastors and church members alike. The burden for change cannot be left to clergy alone. Church members must become voices for morality, ethical behavior, and good examples for children. We need to return to God and make him our only God.

1 AND 2 KINGS: *Leaders and Followers—Failed and Faithful*

QUESTIONS

1. Would you treat your closest relatives the same way Asa treated his mother in 1 Kings 15:13? How far should we go in maintaining positive relationships with people, even our family members, when they hold differing moral values?

2. What would we need to do to help our community turn to God and God's way?

3. Why do you think Asa failed to completely remove the "high places"?

4. Ahab was the worst of all the kings of Israel. Why do people tolerate and even support bad leaders?

5. In what ways can the church offer a positive model for a society that exhibits little dependence upon God?

Prophets at Work

UNIT THREE

1 Kings 17–2 Kings 8

In 1 Kings 17 through 2 Kings 8 we find incidents concerning two of Israel's greatest prophets—Elijah and Elisha—plus a lesser-known but courageous prophet named Micaiah. Their efforts served as a counterweight to the failed and faithless national rulers during this time.

Elijah was the model of the ideal prophet in the minds of New Testament writers. People compared John the Baptist to Elijah (see Malachi 4:5; Luke 1:17), and he appeared in the transfiguration with Moses to speak with Jesus (see Mark 9:2–8).

Lessons five and six contrast the enormous faith of Elijah with the fear and depression that followed. Elijah stood boldly in front of a hostile crowd, challenging false prophets to a public contest. He won! The next day, a hostile queen sent him a message to get out of town by sundown or he was a dead man. He left! He ran miles and miles into the desert. We'll discover the tenderness with which the Lord dealt with his servant, revitalizing him to return to the battle.

The prophet Micaiah is less well-known than Elijah. In the Scripture passage we will study in lesson seven about Micaiah, he was the only prophet to stand up to King Ahab. All the rest of the 400 prophets proclaimed what Ahab wanted to hear—victory. Micaiah insisted on consulting the Lord and proclaiming what the Lord had to say. The word of the Lord predicted doom if Israel and Judah attacked. Guess which prophecy came true.

Elisha succeeded Elijah in the role of premier prophet. Many of the biblical accounts about Elisha involve conflict between Israel and Syria. His ability to visualize things spiritually characterized his ministry. In our lesson about Elisha, lesson eight, we find his reputation in

1 AND 2 KINGS: *Leaders and Followers—Failed and Faithful*

the enemy's country to be strong and positive. Elisha's reputation led a Syrian general named Naaman to seek the prophet to heal his leprosy.

Elijah, Elisha, and Micaiah likely ministered around 850 B.C. They preached in the Northern kingdom of Israel. The Northern kingdom always had two strikes against it spiritually because none of their kings destroyed the two temples with idols in Bethel and Dan that Jeroboam had erected when the nation was founded (1 Kings 12:28–30).[1]

UNIT THREE. PROPHETS AT WORK (1 KINGS 17—2 KINGS 8)

Lesson 5	A Call to Full Commitment	1 Kings 18:1–2, 17–39
Lesson 6	Time to Listen	1 Kings 19:1–18
Lesson 7	Speaking Truth to Power—Alone	1 Kings 22:6–28
Lesson 8	Extending God's Help to a "Foreigner"	2 Kings 5:1–19a

NOTES

1. Unless otherwise indicated, all quotations of Scripture in this unit are from the New International Version.

Focal Text
1 Kings 18:1–2, 17–39

Background
1 Kings 17—18

Main Idea
God calls for our full commitment to him instead of to any other god, including the god of easy success.

Question to Explore
What are the gods of easy success—like Baal—of our day?

Study Aim
To commit myself fully to the true God

Study and Action Emphases
- Affirm the Bible as our authoritative guide for life and ministry
- Share the gospel with all people
- Develop a growing, vibrant faith
- Equip people for servant leadership

LESSON FIVE: A Call to Full Commitment

Quick Read
Elijah exhibited great faith and courage to trust God in a showdown before Ahab and 450 prophets of Baal. God also will enable *us* to meet great challenges.

57

1 AND 2 KINGS: *Leaders and Followers—Failed and Faithful*

Some years ago, the church I served as pastor experienced great revival. During that renewal weekend, 400 people came on Friday night, more than twice the average Sunday School attendance. About 300 people came on Saturday night, and I saw dozens remain in the auditorium into the night, praying as families and as individuals. Two weeks later a man was saved during the offering!

Most of those strongly affected in those days were Christians, even mature Christians, whom God gave a fresh experience with him. I could see the impact years later in lives that truly were changed. From time to time, each of us needs to renew and deepen our commitment to Christ.

In this lesson, we will see the public faith of Elijah calling Israel back to its basic commitment to serve the Lord.

1 Kings 18:1-2, 17-39

¹After a long time, in the third year, the word of the LORD came to Elijah: "Go and present yourself to Ahab, and I will send rain on the land." ²So Elijah went to present himself to Ahab. Now the famine was severe in Samaria. . . .

. . . .

¹⁷When he saw Elijah, he said to him, "Is that you, you troubler of Israel?"

¹⁸"I have not made trouble for Israel," Elijah replied. "But you and your father's family have. You have abandoned the LORD's commands and have followed the Baals. ¹⁹Now summon the people from all over Israel to meet me on Mount Carmel. And bring the four hundred and fifty prophets of Baal and the four hundred prophets of Asherah, who eat at Jezebel's table."

²⁰So Ahab sent word throughout all Israel and assembled the prophets on Mount Carmel. ²¹Elijah went before the people and said, "How long will you waver between two opinions? If the LORD is God, follow him; but if Baal is God, follow him." But the people said nothing.

²²Then Elijah said to them, "I am the only one of the LORD's prophets left, but Baal has four hundred and fifty prophets. ²³Get two bulls for us. Let them choose one for themselves, and let them cut it into pieces and put it on the wood but not set fire to it. I will prepare the other bull and put it on the wood but not set fire to it. ²⁴Then you call on the name of your god, and I will call on the name of the LORD. The god who answers by fire—he is God."

Then all the people said, "What you say is good."

25Elijah said to the prophets of Baal, "Choose one of the bulls and prepare it first, since there are so many of you. Call on the name of your god, but do not light the fire." **26**So they took the bull given them and prepared it.

Then they called on the name of Baal from morning till noon. "O Baal, answer us!" they shouted. But there was no response; no one answered. And they danced around the altar they had made.

27At noon Elijah began to taunt them. "Shout louder!" he said. "Surely he is a god! Perhaps he is deep in thought, or busy, or traveling. Maybe he is sleeping and must be awakened." **28**So they shouted louder and slashed themselves with swords and spears, as was their custom, until their blood flowed. **29**Midday passed, and they continued their frantic prophesying until the time for the evening sacrifice. But there was no response, no one answered, no one paid attention.

30Then Elijah said to all the people, "Come here to me." They came to him, and he repaired the altar of the Lord, which was in ruins. **31**Elijah took twelve stones, one for each of the tribes descended from Jacob, to whom the word of the Lord had come, saying, "Your name shall be Israel." **32**With the stones he built an altar in the name of the Lord, and he dug a trench around it large enough to hold two seahs of seed. **33**He arranged the wood, cut the bull into pieces and laid it on the wood. Then he said to them, "Fill four large jars with water and pour it on the offering and on the wood."

34"Do it again," he said, and they did it again.

"Do it a third time," he ordered, and they did it the third time. **35**The water ran down around the altar and even filled the trench.

36At the time of sacrifice, the prophet Elijah stepped forward and prayed: "O Lord, God of Abraham, Isaac and Israel, let it be known today that you are God in Israel and that I am your servant and have done all these things at your command. **37**Answer me, O Lord, answer me, so these people will know that you, O Lord, are God, and that you are turning their hearts back again."

38Then the fire of the Lord fell and burned up the sacrifice, the wood, the stones and the soil, and also licked up the water in the trench.

39When all the people saw this, they fell prostrate and cried, "The Lord—he is God! The Lord—he is God!"

Background: Elijah Gets Ahab's Attention (17:1–24)

With a clear blue sky as a backdrop, Elijah walked into King Ahab's court and said, "There will be neither dew nor rain in the next few years except at my word" (1 Kings 17:1). Then Elijah simply walked out and disappeared into the countryside.

I can imagine the incident becoming an *in* joke in Israel. People may have nudged each other as the drought began, saying, *It's just Elijah, you know,* and not believing. But as time went on, Ahab began more and more desperately to try to find Elijah, and he could not.

Meanwhile, Elijah had left the country and had found refuge in Zarephath, north of Israel in Phoenicia. God had miraculously fed him and the widow and her family who had given him sanctuary. The drought went on unrelieved for two years. By the time Elijah came back, the king would be ready to listen.

> What fictional gods tempt us?

Elijah Returns (18:1–2)

Two full years had passed. Drought and its partner, famine, had set in. In the third year, the Lord told Elijah to return. When he did, God would send rain, relieving the drought and famine. Note that quite simply Elijah obeyed and went to seek out Ahab. How often do we modern Christians follow the Spirit's guidance so easily? Note also that God acted to save his people on this occasion even when his people didn't know they needed saving. He moved to save them from idolatry, far more serious than the drought.

On the way, Elijah met Obadiah, Ahab's right-hand man. In spite of his official relationship to Ahab, though, Obadiah was faithful to the Lord and not Baal. On one occasion he had protected a hundred prophets by hiding them in caves (18:3–6). Obadiah was terrified when he met Elijah. He was afraid that if he—Obadiah—reported the sighting to the king, Elijah would disappear, and the king would be furious. Elijah reassured him and directed him to tell Ahab he was on his way.

> From time to time, each of us needs to renew and deepen our commitment to Christ.

Confrontation and Challenge (18:17–20)

When Ahab met Elijah, Ahab asked a classic question and received a classic answer. "Is that you, you troubler of Israel?" (18:17), the king shot forth. With no hesitation Elijah fired back, *Oh no, Ahab. You have it backwards. I'm not the one troubling Israel. You are. You and your father's whole family. You've ignored God's commands. You've worshiped the false gods.* By "troubler," the two men were referring to the person who was causing the drought. Ahab accused Elijah. But the prophet knew he hadn't caused it. The Lord had brought judgment, and Elijah had announced it.

Elijah then moved to settle the issue. *Now I challenge you to a showdown. Call all of the prophets of Baal and those of his consort Asherah that your wife Jezebel favors. Collect them at Mount Carmel, and we'll see who's the God of Israel.* (See the small article titled "Baal.") The king obeyed the prophet (a miracle in itself), and 850 prophets and other onlookers gathered on Mount Carmel.

Carmel projected out into the Mediterranean Sea. The area had been disputed between Israel and Phoenecia. Since Baal was a primary god of the latter country, it was appropriate to do spiritual battle between the two gods on that overlapping territory. The situation causes us to ask, *In what ways does our spiritual life overlap the culture of our times? Which one wins—the culture or your spiritual life?*

A Magnificent Challenge (18:21–24)

Elijah challenged the multitude for a clear decision, asking (18:21), "How long will you waver between two opinions?" The word translated "waver" means *to limp* and is the same word translated "danced" in verse 26. Quite possibly, the priests of Baal had a ritual that involved a kind of dance. Elijah pictured all Israel limping about in a strange little dance, trying to seek support from both gods. The prophet said, *You can't do that. Only one god is God. Choose and serve only him.*

Then Elijah proposed a test. Each side would offer a sacrifice laid on an altar with wood piled beneath it. Should one god or the other answer with fire, setting ablaze the sacrifice, then let Israel serve that God and only that God.

Baal Takes His Turn (18:25–29)

The prophets of Baal went first. They killed a bull and laid it on the altar, with kindling beneath. Then they began to pray to Baal to demonstrate his power. (Note that Baal was a storm god, among other things.) Their prayers included ritual limp-dancing. (There's that word again.) The Bible notes the very sad truth: "There was no response; no one answered" (18:26).

Jokes picture calling heaven and being put on hold or routed through an infinite automated menu: *for sickness, press one; for trouble, press two.* Jokes that use such ideas are jokes precisely because God always hears and always responds instantly. But our modern equivalents of Baal never respond, because *there is no Baal.* What fictional gods tempt us?

Do you ever hear spectators *trash-talking* at a ball game? If you're at a baseball game, you may hear spectators yelling things like, *He can't hit.* Or, *Knock it out of the park; he can't pitch.* Elijah's next statements remind me of just that kind of taunting. "Shout louder!" he said. Referring to Baal, Elijah continued, ". . . Perhaps he is deep in thought, or busy, or traveling. Maybe he is sleeping and must be awakened" (18:27). The cutting remarks motivated the prophets of Baal to greater effort. They began trying to attract Baal's attention by cutting themselves. They continued yelling and dancing all afternoon (18:28–29).

> . . . Elijah called Israel to make a choice. . . .

The Lord Claims His People (18:30–39)

Finally, Elijah claimed his turn. He gathered the people and rebuilt an old, ruined altar to the true Lord. Perhaps followers of Baal had become

Baal

The word *Baal* means *lord*. Humans can be lords, but the use in this lesson refers to the god Baal. Principally, he seems to have been a storm god and a fertility god, although he had other manifestations as well. He had a wife, or consort, named Asherah. Originally a Phoenecian god, Baal became popular in Israel due to Jezebel's political marriage to Ahab.

Fertility religions believed in sympathetic magic. Thus, if a couple mated in a temple near the fields, their coupling would stimulate the crops to do likewise and produce an abundant harvest. Likewise, as a storm god, Baal would be expected to win the fireless sacrifice, since storms and lightning were his domain.

so strong in the region that they had destroyed the structure. Now the prophet replaced the altar of Baal with one to the true Lord.

Around the restored altar Elijah dug a trench. When the sacrifice was ready, he had them drench it with twelve jars of water (four jars times three pourings). There was so much water, it ran into the trench, filling it (18:30–35)!

The great prophet's prayer was short. No dancing, cutting, or screaming. Just a brief prayer (18:36–37). God answered instantly and dramatically. Elijah's prayer began by linking the present occasion with the fathers of Israel: Abraham, Isaac, and Israel (Jacob). We too share that continuity through Christ to Elijah, to Moses, to Abraham. The God we worship today was also active in Abraham's day! In fact, God's covenant with Abraham continues to work in the lives of his descendants, the people of Israel and the Christian church.

> *God answered instantly and dramatically.*

In his prayer, Elijah also wanted the Lord to confirm him as his prophet. Elijah had been abused and certainly wanted vindication. More important, he wanted the authority to set things right by casting out the worshipers of Baal.

Quite simply, the Scripture says fire fell and burned up the sacrifice and everything else, even licking up the water in the trench (18:38). Sometimes skeptics say the water attracted lightning. Good thought, but where did the lightning come from? The sky was clear, remember? The Bible clearly means that God sent the fire to prove he was indeed the true Lord of Israel.

> *This story of Elijah illustrates the Lord's superiority over Baal and any other god.*

The people responded (18:39), "The LORD—he is God!" Their faith came first from fear. History shows their faith was short-lived, but it was real for a while. Elijah took advantage of the opportunity to purge the country of idolatry.

Follow-up: Victory and Rain (18:40–46)

Immediately after the thunderous roar from the crowd, Elijah ordered the prophets of Baal to be seized. The crowd overwhelmed them, carried them away from the altar site, and put them to death.

1 AND 2 KINGS: *Leaders and Followers—Failed and Faithful*

Prophets

In the Old Testament, the concept of prophets is quite broad. There were groups of prophets, such as those of Baal and the group of prophets ("company") that followed Elijah to the Jordan on his last day (2 Kings 2:7). Other prophets stood out as individuals, of whom Elijah is the prime example.

Prophets were chosen by God to proclaim what God revealed to them. They announced, explained, and demanded obedience to the word of God. At times, foretelling was a part of the prophet's message. But the main emphasis was always on telling forth the message of God and warning of danger if that message was not obeyed.

Then Elijah told Ahab he could break his fast (18:41). (Fasting was a common practice before interceding with a god.) While Ahab ate, Elijah climbed to the top of Mount Carmel and bent over in prayer. As he prayed, he sent his servant time and again to watch for God's answer. Finally, on the seventh trip, the servant came back to say he saw a cloud the size of a man's hand. Elijah then sent word to Ahab to head for the house before he got drenched and his chariot became stuck in the mud. The sky drew dark and rain fell!

Remember that Kings was originally one book that ended as the nation of Judah was being destroyed and carried into captivity. The book traces the history of why this tragedy occurred. Psalm 137 states the basic problem confronting the captives. "How can we sing the songs of the Lord while in a foreign land?" (Psalm 137:4). Most defeated nations at that time would assume they lost because their local god was defeated by a stronger god. So they had no hesitation trading the weaker god for the stronger god. But Israel interpreted its fall differently. Their destruction came as a punishment for sin. Kings cites chapter and verse of those sins. Further, the book portrays God as the Lord of the whole earth, including Babylon. This story of Elijah illustrates the Lord's superiority over Baal and any other god.

> *To follow Christ means to follow his teachings, and those teachings challenge every human culture.*

Applications and Actions

Ahab and Israel were prisoners of their culture and history. Years earlier, Jereboam I had set up two temples with idols to compete with Jerusalem (1 Kings 12:28–30). No one had corrected that direct breaking of the second commandment. Instead, they had allowed Baal worship from the native Canaanites to creep into their lives. We too inherit a culture that takes many things for granted. Television and other media constantly surround us with values that we unconsciously—or consciously—absorb. To follow Christ means to follow his teachings, and those teachings challenge every human culture.

Like Joshua centuries earlier (Joshua 24:15), Elijah called Israel to make a choice: Baal or God. From time to time we need to face the reality of our own drifting or rebellion. At such a time we need to remember from whence we have fallen, repent, and move closer to our Lord.

QUESTIONS

1. Elijah put his faith on the line by publicly challenging 450 prophets of Baal. How far would you go in standing for your commitment to God?

2. How would you translate Baal worship to the twenty-first century? What are the equivalents of Baal today?

3. How can we as churches and individuals counter the sinful influences of our culture?

Focal Text
1 Kings 19:1–18

Background
1 Kings 19

Main Idea
Even though serving God may be so discouraging and even threatening that we want to give up, we must continue to listen to God and be faithful.

Question to Explore
Are you listening to what God is saying to you right now?

Study Aim
To consider how God is calling me to be faithful to him in spite of the discouragement I may feel

Study and Action Emphases
- Affirm the Bible as our authoritative guide for life and ministry
- Develop a growing, vibrant faith
- Equip people for servant leadership

LESSON SIX
Time to Listen

Quick Read
Elijah fled from Jezebel to Mount Sinai, where he received a fresh encounter with the Lord and a new commission.

1 AND 2 KINGS: *Leaders and Followers—Failed and Faithful*

Do you recall the time of church renewal and revival I described at the beginning of lesson five? During that time, younger adults made one comment over and over about a helpful discovery they had made in their lay renewal weekend groups at that time. (I heard this same comment in years to follow in groups in other churches.) These groups had been chosen randomly, and each group included adults of all age groups.

The younger adults had discovered in these groups that older Christians, whom they had admired and looked up to, also sometimes had problems with their Christian faith and life. These younger adults told of finding this discovery encouraging because they had envied those older believers their ability to appear to live without difficulties. Because their elders could progress in their Christian lives in spite of troubles of various kinds, these younger adults found hope for their own problems. Consider Elijah, who needed encouragement and hope even though he was a prophet of God.

1 Kings 19:1–18

¹Now Ahab told Jezebel everything Elijah had done and how he had killed all the prophets with the sword. ²So Jezebel sent a messenger to Elijah to say, "May the gods deal with me, be it ever so severely, if by this time tomorrow I do not make your life like that of one of them."

³Elijah was afraid and ran for his life. When he came to Beersheba in Judah, he left his servant there, ⁴while he himself went a day's journey into the desert. He came to a broom tree, sat down under it and prayed that he might die. "I have had enough, Lord," he said. "Take my life; I am no better than my ancestors." ⁵Then he lay down under the tree and fell asleep.

All at once an angel touched him and said, "Get up and eat." ⁶He looked around, and there by his head was a cake of bread baked over hot coals, and a jar of water. He ate and drank and then lay down again.

⁷The angel of the Lord came back a second time and touched him and said, "Get up and eat, for the journey is too much for you." ⁸So he got up and ate and drank. Strengthened by that food, he traveled forty days and forty nights until he reached Horeb, the mountain of God. ⁹There he went into a cave and spent the night.

And the word of the Lord came to him: "What are you doing here, Elijah?"

¹⁰ He replied, "I have been very zealous for the Lord God Almighty. The Israelites have rejected your covenant, broken down your altars, and put your prophets to death with the sword. I am the only one left, and now they are trying to kill me too."
¹¹ The Lord said, "Go out and stand on the mountain in the presence of the Lord, for the Lord is about to pass by."
Then a great and powerful wind tore the mountains apart and shattered the rocks before the Lord, but the Lord was not in the wind. After the wind there was an earthquake, but the Lord was not in the earthquake. ¹² After the earthquake came a fire, but the Lord was not in the fire. And after the fire came a gentle whisper. ¹³ When Elijah heard it, he pulled his cloak over his face and went out and stood at the mouth of the cave.
Then a voice said to him, "What are you doing here, Elijah?"
¹⁴ He replied, "I have been very zealous for the Lord God Almighty. The Israelites have rejected your covenant, broken down your altars, and put your prophets to death with the sword. I am the only one left, and now they are trying to kill me too."
¹⁵ The Lord said to him, "Go back the way you came, and go to the Desert of Damascus. When you get there, anoint Hazael king over Aram. ¹⁶ Also, anoint Jehu son of Nimshi king over Israel, and anoint Elisha son of Shaphat from Abel Meholah to succeed you as prophet. ¹⁷ Jehu will put to death any who escape the sword of Hazael, and Elisha will put to death any who escape the sword of Jehu. ¹⁸ Yet I reserve seven thousand in Israel—all whose knees have not bowed down to Baal and all whose mouths have not kissed him."

Overview of 1 Kings 19

In this lesson, we will discover that Elijah also could crash emotionally and spiritually. In lesson five, we saw him bold and courageous, challenging 850 prophets of Baal and Asherah to an incredible test before a crowd of people. He won! This week, we find that a message from a pagan queen dropped him to a spiritual low and sent him running in fear and discouragement miles into the desert.

But the Lord was tender, gently caring for his servant Elijah and allowing him to rest. Finally God appeared to Elijah in a fresh experience that ended with a new commission and work to do.

Elijah Flees Jezebel's Threats (19:1 – 9a)

When King Ahab told his wife Jezebel that all the prophets of Baal and Asherah, whom she worshiped, had been killed (1 Kings 18:40), she was furious. She sent Elijah a message that amounted to, *Get out of town by sundown, or you're a dead man.* In the Greek translation of the Old Testament, she prefaced her threat with the words, *As sure as you are Elijah and I am Jezebel.* Yet, she must have been weakened by Elijah's victory or limited in some other way since she only sent a threat. She apparently was unable to dispatch assassins to kill him on the spot.

> God appeared to Elijah in a fresh experience that ended with a new commission and work to do.

We might expect the one who had been so brave at Carmel on the previous day merely to laugh at such a threat. Instead, Elijah panicked. He ran for his life from Israel to the south of Judah, to Beersheba. The authority of Ahab and Jezebel stopped there at the border of Judah. Elijah left his servant and traveled alone into the wild desert, where years later Jesus would face Satan's temptations.

Elijah came to rest under a "broom tree" (19:4). This bush can reach ten feet in height, but it still does not provide much shade from desert heat. Even so, a small bush beats the direct sun.

Elijah felt spiritually and emotionally broken and alone. In today's parlance, Elijah had *had it*. He called on God to kill him, for he felt worthless (19:4). He felt that although he was still alive, his work would not last. He felt he might as well be dead, as his ancestors were. After expressing these feelings, he fell asleep.

> Do you have a special place and time in your spiritual life in which God has seemed most real to you?

But the Lord was not through with Elijah. An angel awoke the prophet and gave him food and water. Then Elijah went back to sleep. Once again the angel awoke him and fed him, telling him he must have strength for the coming journey (19:7). The Bible frequently shows angels intervening between God and humans. Strengthened by the food, Elijah rose and traveled almost the length of the Sinai peninsula to the site of Mount Horeb (also called Sinai). He found a cave and went in to spend the night (19:8–9).

Horeb was the place Moses met the Lord in a burning bush and received his commission to free his people from Egypt (Exodus 3:1). Later, Moses led the new nation back to the foot of the same mountain, also called Sinai (Exod. 19:1–2). Still later, as Moses received the law and then discovered Israel's rebellion over the golden calf (Exod. 32), Moses asked God to give him a fresh experience of God's presence (Exod. 33:18–23). The Lord kept his promise, renewing Moses' faith and enthusiasm with an experience much like Elijah's. Do you have a special place and time in your spiritual life in which God has seemed most real to you?

God Gives Elijah a Fresh Experience (19:9b–13)

Depression and burn-out often leads to a *pity-party*. Over and over, one repeats to himself or herself the same complaint, perhaps reviewing the mistreatment that has been experienced. It was so with Elijah.

The Lord finally approached his prophet, "What are you doing here, Elijah?" (1 Kings 19:9). Perhaps the Lord was asking, *Why are you outside the territory I assigned to you?* The prophet answered with his complaints. He said he had been faithful to the Lord, but all the rest of Israel had deserted God, killed the prophets, and left only him. He totally ignored his great victory of a few days before and the destruction of the prophets of Baal.

The Lord can speak to a person in the quietness of daily life.

The Lord told Elijah to walk outside the cave on the mountain. Then came a powerful wind that hurled rocks and split them. But Elijah did not sense the presence of God in that wind.

Remnant

In 1 Kings 19:18 the Lord spoke of 7,000 whom he had "reserved" as faithful. Whenever God sends judgment, he never wipes out all his people. A faithful group remains. During the Babylonian exile, many remained faithful. Daniel and Esther portrayed this loyalty in striking ways. In Ezra and Nehemiah we see the remnant returning to Jerusalem and Judea. The Bible always sees the existence of a remnant as being at God's initiative, indicating God's faithfulness to the covenant he made with Abraham and all Israel. The remnant idea culminates most clearly in Jesus' being "obedient to death—even death on a cross" (Philippians 2:8). Reduced to the one man, Jesus, the remnant idea then begins to expand again through the mission of the church.

Next the ground shook violently, but Elijah did not sense God's presence in the earthquake. Then a fire exploded around him, and yet no word from God was in the fire. At last, in the silence, Elijah heard a "gentle whisper." Another translation of the Hebrew is *a sound of fine silence*. Yes, it's a contradiction. But it points to the tremendous difference between a noisome display of power and the quiet voice of God.

> The world is different when a person has experienced God.

The Lord was telling Elijah that he did not always reveal himself in great displays of power as he had at Carmel. Rather when one becomes quiet, one can also hear the voice of God. "Be still, and know that I am God" (Psalm 46:10). The Lord can speak to a person in the quietness of daily life.

A New Commission (19:14–18)

When Elijah experienced God's presence, he wrapped his cloak around his face as if to protect himself from too much exposure to the Lord (19:13). Again God asked Elijah why he was there. Again Elijah repeated his litany of complaints, but I suspect he did so with much less conviction this time. The world is different when a person has experienced God.

The Lord had refreshed his servant with rest, food, exercise (all that running and walking!), and a dynamic personal experience of the presence of God. Now the Lord completed the renewal by giving Elijah his marching orders. First, he allowed the prophet to express his complaints one more time.

Elijah felt that all his work had been for naught. He had been extremely zealous in the Lord's service. Yet all Israel had deserted the Lord. They

Geography and Maps

Understanding the geography of the biblical world helps us better understand the events. For example, if you trace the various locations in the lessons of the last two weeks, you can better appreciate the territory Elijah covered. The action moves from Sidon north of Israel through Carmel to Horeb, miles south of Israel. Perhaps your Bible contains maps. Some Bible atlases and dictionaries have pictures of these areas. If you have access to online maps, such as Google Earth, you can zoom in and get the feel of such rugged territory.

had forgotten and rebelled against the ancient covenant made at Sinai to worship only the Lord. They had replaced the altars of the true God with worship places dedicated to the false gods, the Baals. Those prophets who had spoken against these trends had been persecuted, even killed. Elijah was sure he was the only one left, and Jezebel was trying to exterminate him. Certainly the prophet was mostly correct in his accusations, but in his depression he exaggerated the situation. He had, in fact, won a notable victory for the God of Israel.

The Lord now gave him a new assignment. God sent him from the wilderness of Sinai to the wilderness of Damascus. Part of his commission, later carried out by Elisha, was to anoint Hazael king over Syria and Jehu king over Israel. The Lord also had selected Elisha as Elijah's successor and ordered Elijah to anoint that prophet as well.

In 2 Kings 8:7–15, we find Elisha later carrying out this command by setting up Hazael to become king over Syria. The result for Israel would be terrible, for Hazael brought judgment on Israel. Elisha also anointed Jehu by proxy as king of Israel, sending "a man from the company of the prophets" (2 Kings 9:1). The actual human agent had less importance, for the reality was the Lord was anointing Jehu (2 Kings 9:1–6.).

Who has never grown discouraged?

After giving the instructions to Elijah, then the Lord told him in no uncertain terms that he was not alone. God had preserved 7,000 in Israel who were still faithful to him. They had not participated in any way in Baal worship. Verse 18 states God's determination to "reserve" a remnant. (See the small article, "Remnant.") The Lord would not allow the faith of Israel to disappear.

Implications and Actions

Who has never grown discouraged? To feel guilty about feeling frustrated only adds to the depression. Many Christians have invested so much of themselves in an effort that when the project was over, they crashed. They may have crashed harder if the events did not seem to succeed. Even with success, the sudden shift to less activity can give a sense of burn-out.

Note that the Lord did not attack Elijah or lay a *guilt trip* on him. Rather God provided opportunity to meet the prophet's need for escape, rest, and a fresh commitment. So when you become discouraged, allow

Crossing the Valleys

Tips for walking through depression:
1. Seek companionship. Share your feelings with a trusted friend.
2. Keep a journal. Write down your feelings and thoughts, both positive and negative.
3. Allow yourself to rest. Get extra sleep. Read a novel. Take a trip to a fun place.
4. Be honest with God in your prayers. Tell God how you feel. Then listen for the answer.
5. Get in touch with your mission in life. What life purposes has God given you? Jot down ways you can begin to carry them out again.

---

yourself time to rest and refresh your spirit. Perhaps you can shift some of the time and energy back to Bible study and prayer.

Note also that God gave Elijah new relationships to cure his loneliness. Perhaps in your activity you may have had less time for closeness to friends and family. Depressed folk tend to shut themselves away from people—a mistake. Instead reach out to others and accept their approaches. Perhaps the Lord is giving you new friends as he gave Elisha to Elijah. Likewise, you might stand beside another in friendship as he or she goes through a burn-out period.

Finally, seek a new commission from God, a new experience of God. The Lord is not through with you. Discovering a new sense of purpose will carry you forward in joy.

Discovering a new sense of purpose will carry you forward in joy.

Lesson 6: Time to Listen

QUESTIONS:

1. How do you relate to Elijah's spiritual and emotional crash? Do you frequently find yourself feeling low? Does guilt overwhelm you at these moments? What does Elijah's experience have to teach you?

2. How do you react to disappointments and spiritual weariness? How do those feelings affect your relation to God?

3. Who is in your network of supporters who will accompany you through your troubles? Who are the friends with whom you can share your inmost feelings and from whom you can receive strength?

4. What sense of direction and purpose do you have in your life? Is that direction in response to a call from God?

Focal Text
1 Kings 22:6–28

Background
1 Kings 22

Main Idea
Being faithful to God means speaking God's truth to power even when to do so is lonely and dangerous.

Question to Explore
What does it take to speak truth to power, especially when you must stand alone?

Study Aim
To identify qualities in Micaiah that enabled him to speak truth to power and commit myself to greater faithfulness in speaking God's truth today

Study and Action Emphases
- Affirm the Bible as our authoritative guide for life and ministry
- Share the gospel with all people
- Develop a growing, vibrant faith
- Equip people for servant leadership

LESSON SEVEN

Speaking Truth to Power—Alone

Quick Read
The prophet Micaiah, speaking for the Lord, courageously told King Ahab news he did not want to hear in spite of 400 other prophets foretelling the exact opposite conclusion.

1 AND 2 KINGS: *Leaders and Followers—Failed and Faithful*

The city was in crisis. Scandals were battering city hall. Race relations were at a low ebb, and the economy was taking a hit from a diminishing oil and gas industry. At that time, the pastor of one of the leading churches in the city launched a series of sermons aimed at the crisis. The newspaper quoted the pastor as saying, "History is littered with the wreckage of once-proud cities that shut their door to surprises. Jesus uttered woes against specific cities for their refusal to change in the face of a New Age, and he will do no less to [our city] if we worship the idolatrous god of the status quo."[1] The sermon series made the front page of the newspaper and was reported around the state. People in the city talked about those messages delivered from the pulpit of the First Baptist Church, and the sermons made a difference.

Let us consider our own challenges to faithfulness. How can we face them with courage, even if we must do so alone? Furthermore, how does a sincere Christian decide when the Lord is leading and when the impulse may come from other motivations? This week's study can point us toward answers. Laypeople as well as pastors need them.

1 Kings 22:6–28

⁶So the king of Israel brought together the prophets—about four hundred men—and asked them, "Shall I go to war against Ramoth Gilead, or shall I refrain?"

"Go," they answered, "for the Lord will give it into the king's hand."

⁷But Jehoshaphat asked, "Is there not a prophet of the LORD here whom we can inquire of?"

⁸The king of Israel answered Jehoshaphat, "There is still one man through whom we can inquire of the LORD, but I hate him because he never prophesies anything good about me, but always bad. He is Micaiah son of Imlah."

"The king should not say that," Jehoshaphat replied.

⁹So the king of Israel called one of his officials and said, "Bring Micaiah son of Imlah at once."

¹⁰Dressed in their royal robes, the king of Israel and Jehoshaphat king of Judah were sitting on their thrones at the threshing floor by the entrance of the gate of Samaria, with all the prophets prophesying before them. ¹¹Now Zedekiah son of Kenaanah had made iron horns and he declared, "This is what the LORD says: 'With these you will gore the Arameans until they are destroyed.'"

¹²All the other prophets were prophesying the same thing. "Attack Ramoth Gilead and be victorious," they said, "for the Lord will give it into the king's hand."

¹³The messenger who had gone to summon Micaiah said to him, "Look, as one man the other prophets are predicting success for the king. Let your word agree with theirs, and speak favorably."

¹⁴But Micaiah said, "As surely as the Lord lives, I can tell him only what the Lord tells me."

¹⁵When he arrived, the king asked him, "Micaiah, shall we go to war against Ramoth Gilead, or shall I refrain?"

"Attack and be victorious," he answered, "for the Lord will give it into the king's hand."

¹⁶The king said to him, "How many times must I make you swear to tell me nothing but the truth in the name of the Lord?"

¹⁷Then Micaiah answered, "I saw all Israel scattered on the hills like sheep without a shepherd, and the Lord said, 'These people have no master. Let each one go home in peace.'"

¹⁸The king of Israel said to Jehoshaphat, "Didn't I tell you that he never prophesies anything good about me, but only bad?"

¹⁹Micaiah continued, "Therefore hear the word of the Lord: I saw the Lord sitting on his throne with all the host of heaven standing around him on his right and on his left. ²⁰And the Lord said, 'Who will entice Ahab into attacking Ramoth Gilead and going to his death there?'

"One suggested this, and another that. ²¹Finally, a spirit came forward, stood before the Lord and said, 'I will entice him.'

²²'By what means?' the Lord asked.

"'I will go out and be a lying spirit in the mouths of all his prophets,' he said.

"'You will succeed in enticing him,' said the Lord. 'Go and do it.'

²³"So now the Lord has put a lying spirit in the mouths of all these prophets of yours. The Lord has decreed disaster for you."

²⁴Then Zedekiah son of Kenaanah went up and slapped Micaiah in the face. "Which way did the spirit from the Lord go when he went from me to speak to you?" he asked.

²⁵Micaiah replied, "You will find out on the day you go to hide in an inner room."

²⁶The king of Israel then ordered, "Take Micaiah and send him back to Amon the ruler of the city and to Joash the king's son ²⁷and say, 'This is what the king says: Put this fellow in prison and give him nothing but bread and water until I return safely.'"

²⁸Micaiah declared, "If you ever return safely, the Lord has not spoken through me." Then he added, "Mark my words, all you people!"

1 AND 2 KINGS: *Leaders and Followers—Failed and Faithful*

Setting the Scene

In 1 Kings 20 we read of King Ahab leading Israel to defeat Ben-Hadad, king of Aram. As part of the settlement of that war, Ben-Hadad agreed to return control of some cities his father had taken from Omri, Ahab's father. Apparently he had not returned Ramoth-Gilead, probably a border city. Ahab decided to conquer that city and called on Jehoshaphat, king of Judah, to help (1 Kings 22:1–3). Both kings sought assurance of God's approval from a group of 400 prophets. These men told the kings that the Lord would bless their endeavor. This word of assurance was the prelude to the kings' encounter with Micaiah, who had a decidedly different message.

> *What they really sought . . . was rubber-stamping for their plans.*

Popular Prophets (22:6–12)

A seminary professor often told his students, "You can't put God in your pocket." No, you can't, but wealthy and powerful leaders can certainly put prophets, priests, and other ministers in their pockets. Ahab gathered 400 prophets, whom he trusted to support his government at all times.

> *Do we begin meetings with cursory prayers and conclude them asking God to endorse our decisions?*

Who were they? They seem to have been prophets of the Lord. Elijah had led in the killing of the prophets of Baal, although whether the other 400 prophets of Asherah were killed we don't know with certainty (lesson five, 1 Kings 18). Yet references to "the LORD" throughout 1 Kings 22 point to prophets at least nominally committed to God. Zedekiah (see 22:11, 24) was one of these prophets, and his name means *the Lord is my righteousness* (or *my salvation*). But Zedekiah and the others were obviously court prophets, perhaps appointed and subsidized by Ahab.

The 400 prophets told the kings what they wanted to hear. Ahab asked specifically, "Shall I go to war against Ramoth Gilead, or shall I refrain?" (22:6). They unanimously replied, "Go . . . for the Lord will give it into the king's hand" (22:7).

For some reason King Jehoshaphat of Judah wasn't convinced. In spite of the overwhelming support, he asked whether there was yet another

Host

The word "host" (1 Kings 22:19) can have several meanings that may overlap. First, and perhaps most often, "host" points to the armies of God. The expression *the Lord of hosts* thus pictures God as the commander of the heavenly armies (see Psalm 24:10). Second, the word can indicate angels as in Luke's Christmas story (Luke 2:14). Finally the word occasionally seems to refer to a council of heavenly advisors as it does in today's passage.

---

prophet they could call on. Ahab acknowledged there was such a person, but he complained that he hated this prophet because he always prophesied bad news. Jehoshaphat disagreed. "The king should not say that" (22:8). Jehoshaphat apparently felt that all prophets deserved a measure of respect regardless of their message. After all, the king of Judah worshiped in Jerusalem and may have been more receptive to the Lord than the king of Israel, who had inherited the temples at Bethel and Dan, which both exhibited idols. So Ahab sent for Micaiah.

> *. . . This passage warns us of the human tendency to seek our own will before God's.*

Verse 10 tells us that all this took place while both kings sat in royal splendor at the gates of Samaria, Israel's capital. The word translated in most versions as "threshing floor" may mean simply an open public area, beaten down by the traffic through it. The mass of people entering and leaving the city would beat out an area on both sides of the gate.

The prophets were putting on an impressive display before the two kings. Zedekiah did his part with an act of prophetic symbolism. (Prophetic symbolism was a form of prophecy that involved demonstrating the message in a symbolic action. For examples, see Jeremiah 19; Ezekiel 4.) Zedekiah took a pair of iron horns he had made and pretended to be a bull goring a victim. He claimed Israel and Judah would destroy Aram as a horned animal mutilates its target.

Micaiah Begs to Differ (22:13–18)

The messenger who found Micaiah not only delivered the two kings' request to come, but he also gave advice. The messenger told the prophet that all of the other prophets were predicting success in the proposed venture. The courier then recommended Micaiah go along with them and make the same prediction.

Micaiah's answer was brief. *I can say only what the Lord tells me.*

But when Micaiah arrived before the kings and the assembled prophets, he appeared to take the messenger's advice. Ahab asked, "Shall we go to war against Ramoth Gilead, or shall I refrain?" The prophet replied "Attack and be victorious" (22:15).

Perhaps a tone of sarcasm in Micaiah's voice prompted Ahab to pin him down. Ahab said (22:16), "How many times must I make you swear to tell me nothing but the truth in the name of the Lord?" The demand led the seer to report a quite different vision.

Micaiah said he had seen the armies of Israel defeated and scattered. He compared them to sheep without a shepherd. Further, he heard the Lord saying they had "no master. Let each one go home in peace" (22:17). "No master" implied the death of the king.

See, I told you so, said Ahab to Jehoshaphat. The king felt he never heard good news from Micaiah, only bad. Remember that these kings were supposedly seeking divine guidance. What they really sought, though, was rubber-stamping for their plans. How often do we approach decisions like this? Do we begin meetings with cursory prayers and conclude them asking God to endorse our decisions? Perhaps we would do better devoting more of our meetings to prayer for divine guidance.

> *. . . We often are tempted to go along to get along.*

A Lying Spirit (22:19–23)

Apparently sincere, 400 prophets gave a positive response. Only Micaiah spoke negatively. Why the difference? In the past, the 400 must have been right some of the time, or they would have been dismissed and not consulted. Micaiah explained the situation by reporting a revelation.

He had seen a vision of the Lord consulting "with all the host of heaven." (See the small article "Host" for more information.) Here the word "host" appears to refer to a heavenly council. One member is designated a "spirit," and perhaps the others were also.

In this conference, the Lord sought someone to lure Ahab to his death through attacking Ramoth Gilead. Several proposals were made until one

Lesson 7: Speaking Truth to Power—Alone

Seeking God's Will

Consider how many of these suggestions you practice in your life as you seek God's will:
(1) Genuinely seeking God's will rather than your own
(2) Searching the Scriptures
(3) Seeking out people of wisdom
(4) Recalling how God has led you in the past
(5) Praying for God's leadership

---

spirit came forward with a surprising plan. He would go out and become "a lying spirit in the mouths of all his prophets" (22:22). That is, he would induce the 400 not to tell the truth but to report falsehood to Ahab. This plan implies that the prophets did have access to truth but they could be pressured to misrepresent that truth by people in power. The Lord approved the suggestion and said, "Go and do it" (22:22).

What do you think about God's sponsoring "a lying spirit"? One should remember at least two things to think adequately about this event. First, Ahab was generally an enemy of the Lord. He had worshiped Baal and sponsored at least 400 of Baal's prophets. His stealing Naboth's vineyard (1 Kings 21) showed he had little ethics. Second, the Bible pictures God's character as including judgment, not only in the Old Testament, but also in the New. Sometimes that judgment is carried out by other humans.

Jesus Christ is central.

Micaiah's message is summed up in verse 23, "the Lord has put a lying spirit in the mouths of all these prophets of yours. The Lord has decreed disaster for you." Note that Micaiah specified "these prophets of yours." They did not belong to God but to the king. I suspect the lying spirit didn't have to work very hard to accomplish the task.

Backlash (22:24–28)

As Elijah had stood for the Lord before a larger crowd, so Micaiah faced down most of this large group of "prophets." But Zedekiah (he of the iron horns!) was not intimidated but angered. He slapped Micaiah on the face.

The slap communicated both insult and rejection. He felt Micaiah had insulted *him*! Sarcastically he asked (22:24), "Which way did the spirit from the Lord go when he went from me to speak to you?"

Micaiah gave as good as he got. *You'll find out when you run through the house, scrambling to find a safe place to hide.* Then Ahab got into the fray. He turned the prophet over to the city's ruler and the king's own son, Joash. He told them to "put this fellow in prison and give him nothing but bread and water until I return safely" (22:27). As Micaiah was led off, he fired the last shot. "If you ever return safely, the LORD has not spoken through me." Micaiah called on the people to bear witness of his prophecy.

Note that King Ahab was killed in battle as predicted. The Bible does not tell us what became of Micaiah.

> *. . . We often need to devote more time to prayer before we formulate our plans of action.*

Application

First, this passage warns us of the human tendency to seek our own will before God's. Leaders often rationalize what they already plan to do. Even pastors and Christian laypeople can deceive themselves, claiming their plans are God's plans.

Second, we often are tempted to *go along to get along*. A better approach is to "examine the Scriptures every day to see if [something] is true" (Acts 17:11). Individual thought, analysis, and prayer usually lead us safely to God's will.

Third, truth will never contradict the Bible, properly interpreted with the leadership of the Holy Spirit. God is never going to approve adultery, stealing, or murder. Understanding the broad foundations of Scripture guides us to the Lord's will. Jesus Christ is central. So are grace, mercy, forgiveness, and judgment.

Finally, we often need to devote more time to prayer before we formulate our plans of action.

Lesson 7: Speaking Truth to Power—Alone

QUESTIONS

1. Have you or your church had occasion to "speak truth to power"?

2. What situations in your community need a prophet to address them?

3. What local, state, and national issues need to be held up to the standards of the Bible?

4. How do you resolve the conflict when people on both sides of an issue quote Scripture?

NOTES

1. See "Revisiting the Crossroads: How Has Shreveport Changed in 30 Years?" *The Shreveport Times* (September 17, 2006). The pastor was Dr. William Hull.

Focal Text
2 Kings 5:1–19a

Background
2 Kings 2—5

Main Idea
God calls all people to come to him and encourages his servants to offer help to all who come.

Questions to Explore
What needs do you have that you have been unwilling to bring to God? What resources do you have that God wants you to offer to people who are different from you?

Study Aim
To identify needs I have that I should bring to God and God-given resources I have that God wants me to offer to people different from me

Study and Action Emphases
- Affirm the Bible as our authoritative guide for life and ministry
- Share the gospel with all people
- Develop a growing, vibrant faith
- Value all people as created in the image of God
- Obey and serve Jesus by meeting physical, spiritual, and emotional needs
- Equip people for servant leadership

LESSON EIGHT

Extending God's Help to a "Foreigner"

Quick Read
Elisha healed Naaman of leprosy, even though Naaman was from an enemy nation and to that point had worshiped different gods.

1 AND 2 KINGS: *Leaders and Followers—Failed and Faithful*

A young woman went to a birthday party and invited a friend there to visit our church. Another woman heard her and piped up, "Can I come too? Is anyone welcome?"

"Of course," the first replied, "Anyone."

"What about those from other denominations?"

"Sure, come on."

"That comes with fine print, doesn't it. I mean racially."

"It does not! Anyone is welcome at our church. We have greeted those of another race exactly like we greet those like us."

Others at the party began to name people often considered unacceptable by society, even by many church people. "Yes," the young woman replied, "they are welcome, too. The church is not for perfect people. We're all sinners of one kind or another."

The woman concluded her report to me by saying, "I feel our churches should open their arms and show God's love to everyone. If we can't feel loved and welcomed in a church, then something is wrong. After all, a church is supposed to be the house of God, not the house of man."

Another young woman—a girl, really—also understood that God was for everyone. This week we study how a slave pointed her owner to healing back in her own country.

2 Kings 5:1–19a

1 Now Naaman was commander of the army of the king of Aram. He was a great man in the sight of his master and highly regarded, because through him the Lord had given victory to Aram. He was a valiant soldier, but he had leprosy.

2 Now bands from Aram had gone out and had taken captive a young girl from Israel, and she served Naaman's wife. **3** She said to her mistress, "If only my master would see the prophet who is in Samaria! He would cure him of his leprosy."

4 Naaman went to his master and told him what the girl from Israel had said. **5** "By all means, go," the king of Aram replied. "I will send a letter to the king of Israel." So Naaman left, taking with him ten talents of silver, six thousand shekels of gold and ten sets of clothing. **6** The letter that he took to the king of Israel read: "With this letter I am sending my servant Naaman to you so that you may cure him of his leprosy."

7 As soon as the king of Israel read the letter, he tore his robes and said, "Am I God? Can I kill and bring back to life? Why does this fellow send

Lesson 8: Extending God's Help to a "Foreigner"

someone to me to be cured of his leprosy? See how he is trying to pick a quarrel with me!"

⁸When Elisha the man of God heard that the king of Israel had torn his robes, he sent him this message: "Why have you torn your robes? Have the man come to me and he will know that there is a prophet in Israel." ⁹So Naaman went with his horses and chariots and stopped at the door of Elisha's house. ¹⁰Elisha sent a messenger to say to him, "Go, wash yourself seven times in the Jordan, and your flesh will be restored and you will be cleansed."

¹¹But Naaman went away angry and said, "I thought that he would surely come out to me and stand and call on the name of the LORD his God, wave his hand over the spot and cure me of my leprosy. ¹²Are not Abana and Pharpar, the rivers of Damascus, better than any of the waters of Israel? Couldn't I wash in them and be cleansed?" So he turned and went off in a rage.

¹³Naaman's servants went to him and said, "My father, if the prophet had told you to do some great thing, would you not have done it? How much more, then, when he tells you, 'Wash and be cleansed'!" ¹⁴So he went down and dipped himself in the Jordan seven times, as the man of God had told him, and his flesh was restored and became clean like that of a young boy.

¹⁵Then Naaman and all his attendants went back to the man of God. He stood before him and said, "Now I know that there is no God in all the world except in Israel. Please accept now a gift from your servant."

¹⁶The prophet answered, "As surely as the LORD lives, whom I serve, I will not accept a thing." And even though Naaman urged him, he refused.

¹⁷"If you will not," said Naaman, "please let me, your servant, be given as much earth as a pair of mules can carry, for your servant will never again make burnt offerings and sacrifices to any other god but the LORD. ¹⁸But may the LORD forgive your servant for this one thing: When my master enters the temple of Rimmon to bow down and he is leaning on my arm and I bow there also—when I bow down in the temple of Rimmon, may the LORD forgive your servant for this."

¹⁹"Go in peace," Elisha said.

Setting the Scene

Part of Elijah's new assignment from God (1 Kings 19:16) was to anoint Elisha as his successor (see 19:19–21). When Elisha was accompanying his mentor, Elijah, to Elijah's appointment to be translated to heaven in a whirlwind, the older man asked what final blessing he could give the younger. Elisha asked to be Elijah's successor. Elijah replied that if Elisha saw what happened as Elijah was translated, then the Lord had chosen him as his successor.

How often do we imagine how God will act and then are surprised by what God actually does?

Of course, Elisha did see, and God indeed had appointed him (2 Kings 2:10–12). Chapters 2—4 of 2 Kings tell of several miracles Elisha worked that drew attention to him and affirmed his prophetic ministry. Accounts of various incidents in Elisha's ministry extend through 2 Kings 13:20.

Sickness and Witness (5:1–6)

Naaman was "commander of the army of the king of Aram," or Syria, and "highly regarded" (5:1). However, he had come down with a devastating skin disease. Many translations call this disease "leprosy," but leprosy in that day is to be distinguished from our modern Hansen's disease, sometimes known as leprosy. Leprosy in that day may have been any one of several skin diseases. (See the small article "Leprosy" and Leviticus 13—14.)

Naaman's disease was considered highly contagious. If something were not done, he likely would be forced to leave his position, home, and family to live away from those who could catch his sickness. Can you imagine how he felt as he was about to lose his supreme status as general to become a homeless vagabond?

"I feel our churches should open their arms and show God's love to everyone. . . ."

Naaman's wife had a young girl as her handmaid. She was an unnamed slave from Israel who kept her faith and also showed compassion toward her owners. When she heard of Naaman's leprosy, she spoke to his wife, telling her of a prophet in Samaria, Israel's capital. The young Hebrew girl believed Elisha could heal Naaman.

Apparently the general was receptive to his wife and the advice of the young girl. At this point, Naaman was willing to go to great lengths to find healing and preserve his cherished lifestyle.

Before leaving, Naaman sought permission and help from his boss, the king of Aram. The king cooperated and even commanded him to go.

Further, the king offered what we would call a letter of recommendation to the king of Israel. Perhaps he thought the king controlled the prophet. Naaman also carried with him as a gift a huge amount of silver and gold, plus ten sets of clothing. We might compare the latter to ten high-priced suits.

Shock and Prescription (5:7–13)

The king of Israel read the letter from Aram and took offense. He was so upset he tore his robes, a traditional sign of grief. He was no healer. Was Aram trying to provoke an excuse for war? The king believed only God could cure such an illness, and he knew he certainly wasn't divine.

Elisha heard of the king's distress and asked the king to send Naaman to him. No need for the king to get upset. Elisha would demonstrate the power of Israel's God.

Imagine the scene when the general and his entourage of servants and bodyguards pulled up to the door of Elisha's house. Did the prophet sense that another problem of Naaman was his pride? Perhaps so, for Elisha didn't trouble himself to answer the door. Rather he sent a messenger to tell Naaman to go wash himself in the Jordan seven times. He would then be cleansed of his leprosy.

> "Can I come too? Is anyone welcome?"

Naaman's pride erupted. "I thought that he would surely come out to me and stand and call on the name of the LORD his God, wave his hand over the spot and cure me of my leprosy" (5:11). Naaman continued, *If the prophet merely intended to send a messenger telling me to bathe, why couldn't I have washed in a real river—one of those in my home country?* Naaman's

Leprosy

Leprosy appears in the Bible a number of times and is portrayed as being highly contagious and quite serious. Eight hundred years after Elisha, Jesus encountered ten lepers, living outside the city and banded together for mutual help (Luke 17:11–19). Leviticus 13—14 gives various instructions about leprosy. We don't know precisely what the Bible means by leprosy in people, but the reference is most likely to various skin diseases. Leprosy in the Bible is different from our modern Hansen's disease.

pride was offended. He was so offended and angry that he seemed on the verge of going home with his leprosy. How often do we imagine how God will act and then are surprised by what God actually does?

A possible additional element in Naaman's pride and anger is that Naaman may have led the army that defeated the joint forces of Israel and Judah (2 Kings 22). Naaman worshiped the god Rimmon and probably considered him superior to the Lord since, in his mind, Rimmon had defeated the Lord in battle.

> This story reminds us to remember the people we sometimes refer to as the little *people*, people who are easy to miss with our focus on celebrity and power.

But Namaan's servants calmed him down. (Notice the role of servants in this story: the little slave girl, Elisha's messenger, Naaman's servants.) Naaman's servants pointed out that if the prophet had given him an arduous task to perform, he would have done so without question. They had come this far seeking a cure, and it would require little more to follow Elisha's directions.

A Cure, a Gift, and a Conversion (5:13–19)

Naaman accepted the servants' advice, went "down" to the Jordan, and dipped himself seven times into the river waters. (He is described as going "down" because the Jordan flows through a valley, much lower than Samaria, the Northern kingdom, which is in the hill country.) Carrying out the actions the man of God prescribed brought cleansing and healing. Naaman's skin became as clear and smooth as that of "a young boy" (5:14). Note that his pride was gone as well. He returned to Elisha in a very different mood.

This time Elisha met Naaman in person. Elisha had more to teach spiritually. The commander had become a believer in the true God. "Now

How Accepting Is Your Church?

- ❏ All people are greeted and made to feel at home.
- ❏ New members are included quickly in all activities.
- ❏ Exclusive cliques are not allowed to form or are broken up in love.
- ❏ Outreach activities include everyone and exclude no one.

I know that there is no God in all the world except in Israel" (5:15). Then Naaman offered a gift as payment for his newfound health. The Hebrew word translated "gift" means *blessing* (see KJV). Elisha had blessed him, and now the wealthy man wanted to return the favor.

The prophet, though, declared his services to be free "as surely as the LORD lives, whom I serve." This was grace in action. The Lord healed Naaman because he chose to, not because Naaman had earned it or paid for it. Even so, Christ died for our sins while we were still enemies (Romans 5:10).

If Elisha would not accept a large gift, Naaman asked the prophet for a small one. He wanted to carry two mule loads of dirt back to Aram. He vowed to make no future sacrifices to any God but the Lord. Presumably he wanted the earth to form the foundation of a small altar, and so in a sense he would be worshiping on the land of Israel. The request reflects the old idea of a nation's god being tied to the geographical location of the nation. Note also, that the formerly proud Naaman now called himself "your servant," that is, of Elisha, who in turn served the Lord (2 Kings 5:17). Elisha had done more for him spiritually than physically.

Where do you seek solutions to your problems and help in your difficulties?

Then Naaman made a strange request before returning home. After vowing that he personally would make offerings to no god but the Lord, Naaman recognized he would have to go with the king to the temple of Rimmon as part of his ceremonial duties. In the future the trips would be purely ritual for Naaman, not for worship. He wanted Elisha to understand this and wanted Elisha to forgive in advance for any guilt such an action might incur.

Elijah granted his request in the simple words, "Go in peace" (5:19). Perhaps the logic of Elijah's acceptance of Naaman's request was that Naaman was a new convert.

An Unpleasant Afterward (5:19b–27)

Elijah's servant Gehazi got greedy. He pursued Naaman and lied to him about a sudden need that had arisen for two other prophets to have money and clothing. The general graciously granted him the request, which the servant promptly hid in his own house.

But Elisha was a seer, an important role of a prophet. He confronted Gehazi with the news that his spirit had witnessed the whole thing. As a result, the dishonest servant became himself a leper, with that disease being passed to his descendants. It's ironic that the unbeliever Naaman was healed during the story, and the believing Gehazi became a leper.

Attitudes and Actions

1. One reason Naaman received God's blessing was because he asked. Elisha granted his request even though Naaman was an arch-enemy of Israel. Several hundred years later, when the people of Israel (Judah) were in exile, in captivity, Israel would have read this story about Naaman as a reminder that the Lord was the one God of the world.

2. Naaman's taking seven baths was simple. Coaches repeatedly stress the importance of the fundamentals of their sport, even as pastors continually emphasize the basics of prayer and Bible study. These fundamentals are neither difficult nor spectacular. They take only a little time each day. Yet simple, repeated acts often make a huge difference.

3. This story reminds us to remember the people we sometimes refer to as the *little* people, people who are easy to miss with our focus on celebrity and power. The little servant girl set things in motion. Naaman's servants encouraged him to continue on the path to healing. Many people in the Bible likely never knew on earth the good they had done and that their actions were praised in Scripture. Consider the widow who gave her mite. Look at the list of those whom Paul greeted at the end of Romans. They all had a story to tell, but those tales were not collected and passed on. Perhaps your influence is spreading far beyond your imagination.

4. The little girl pointed Naaman to a spiritual healer. Elisha, in turn, not only healed him physically, but treated his spiritual condition as well. Where do you seek solutions to your problems and help in your difficulties? Certainly we should seek the assistance of skilled experts in whatever need we have. We must remember also to seek the Lord.

Lesson 8: Extending God's Help to a "Foreigner"

QUESTIONS

1. How open are you to people who are different from you? How receptive is your church to "outsiders"?

2. Do we have expectations about how God *must* act to meet our needs, leading to disappointment when God seems to act in ways different from what we expect?

3. How well do you and your church include everyone—even the *little* people—in planning and activities?

4. How well do you and your church keep moving toward the goals of God's kingdom?

5. When you face trouble or difficulty in life, do you immediately think of presenting it to God? Or do you feel God is unable to help, doesn't care, or is too busy?

Missing the Last Chance

UNIT FOUR

2 Kings 9–17

Remember that the political unity of the people of God called Israel had ended when Solomon died. From that time two political entities existed, the kingdom of Israel and the kingdom of Judah. The Northern kingdom (Israel) was more unstable because it lacked a strong dynastic family (like that of David). Also it was geographically more exposed to outside influences of both political power and religious corruption.[1]

Second Kings 9—17 continues telling the story of the two kingdoms in its back-and-forth pattern. The two studies in this unit will focus on the kings of Israel rather than Judah in an attempt to understand why God punished the Northern kingdom more than 100 years before Judah experienced a similar fate. The material concerning Israel covers the last sixty to sixty-five years of her national life. The biblical writer is clear in his conviction that God punished Israel because the kings provided poor leadership, spiritual and otherwise, and because the people refused to obey his instructions to them.

When the Assyrians defeated Israel and took some of them into captivity, the Israelites experienced enslavement to another people group for the first time since God had delivered them from Egypt. A key question is whether Judah would learn or benefit from what happened to Israel. We will discover the answer in the unit of study after this one.[2]

1 AND 2 KINGS: *Leaders and Followers—Failed and Faithful*

UNIT FOUR. MISSING THE LAST CHANCE (2 KINGS 9—17)

| Lesson 9 | Drifting Toward Disaster | 2 Kings 14:23–29; 15:8–10, 13–14, 17–30 |
| Lesson 10 | Death of a Nation | 2 Kings 17:1–18, 21–23 |

NOTES

1. Unless otherwise indicated, all Scripture quotations in unit four are from the New International Version.
2. In units four and five I am following the dates for each king as set forth by John Bright, the respected Old Testament scholar, in his book *A History of Israel*, 4th ed. (Louisville, KY: Westminster John Knox Press, 2000). The reader should be aware of serious chronological difficulties one faces in trying to reconcile all of the biblical numbers assigned to the various kings. Surely some of this is due to what we do not know of how ancient Israel considered fractions of years and to their use of a possible system of co-regencies (time in which a son ruled with his father before the latter's death). We can be thankful that the issues of this nature are few in number.

Focal Text

2 Kings 14:23–29; 15:8–10, 13–14, 17–30

Background

2 Kings 14:23–29; 15:8–31

Main Idea

Unstable and unworthy leadership can lead followers to disaster.

Question to Explore

Why is it so dangerous when leadership is unstable and unworthy?

Study Aim

To describe the problems that signaled that Israel was heading toward disaster and to identify implications for our day

Study and Action Emphases

- Affirm the Bible as our authoritative guide for life and ministry
- Develop a growing, vibrant faith
- Equip people for servant leadership

LESSON NINE: Drifting Toward Disaster

Quick Read

The twofold role of godly or spiritual leaders includes providing a positive example of obedience to God and warning followers of the dangers of disobedience.

1 AND 2 KINGS: *Leaders and Followers—Failed and Faithful*

For many years Curtis Ebbesmeyer, an oceanographer in Seattle, Washington, has studied the drift patterns of the Pacific Ocean due to the prevailing currents of water and wind. Several years ago an opportunity to test his theories fell into his lap. The container vessel *Hansa Carrier*, en route from Korea to the United States, encountered a storm. A large wave washed twenty-one shipping containers overboard. Five of them held about 80,000 Nike® shoes. After the big "swoosh" of the wave (pun intended, sorry), four of the five opened into the stormy water, releasing 60,000 shoes.

Less than a year later the shoes began washing ashore onto Canada's Vancouver Island and the beaches of Oregon and Washington. The location where the shoes came ashore generally confirmed the drift patterns Ebbesmeyer had proposed. The shoes did not "drift aimlessly" in the water of the Pacific; rather, they drifted toward land in a predictable pattern.

Such is the nature of drifting, whether it is physical or spiritual in nature. In the ninth century B.C., the Northern kingdom of Israel was drifting toward disaster. They were drifting in that direction for particular reasons. One of those reasons was the conduct of the kings who led them during this period. They neither provided positive leadership nor warned the Israelites of the danger of disobeying God.

Remember that the two previous units focused respectively on the breaking apart of the kingdom of Israel into Israel and Judah (1 Kings 12—16) and the prophetic ministries of Elijah and Elisha to Israel (1 Kings 17—2 Kings 8). Israel needed those prophetic voices because she had become unfaithful to Yahweh, her God.

God was not pleased with Israel and used Elisha to anoint a military commander named Jehu to be the new king of Israel (2 Kings 9:1–10). God used Jehu to judge the evil of the dynasty of Ahab (and Jezebel). Jehu murdered Joram, the king of Israel, and succeeded him. He also killed Jezebel and many prophets of the Canaanite god Baal as well as Ahaziah, the king of Judah. Second Kings 9—14 summarizes the reigns of the kings of Israel and Judah from the rise of Jehu in 842 B.C. through the early years of the eighth century.

2 Kings 14:23–29

²³In the fifteenth year of Amaziah son of Joash king of Judah, Jeroboam son of Jehoash king of Israel became king in Samaria, and he reigned

forty-one years. ²⁴He did evil in the eyes of the Lord and did not turn away from any of the sins of Jeroboam son of Nebat, which he had caused Israel to commit. ²⁵He was the one who restored the boundaries of Israel from Lebo Hamath to the Sea of the Arabah, in accordance with the word of the Lord, the God of Israel, spoken through his servant Jonah son of Amittai, the prophet from Gath Hepher.

²⁶The Lord had seen how bitterly everyone in Israel, whether slave or free, was suffering; there was no one to help them. ²⁷And since the Lord had not said he would blot out the name of Israel from under heaven, he saved them by the hand of Jeroboam son of Jehoash.

²⁸As for the other events of Jeroboam's reign, all he did, and his military achievements, including how he recovered for Israel both Damascus and Hamath, which had belonged to Yaudi, are they not written in the book of the annals of the kings of Israel? ²⁹Jeroboam rested with his fathers, the kings of Israel. And Zechariah his son succeeded him as king.

2 Kings 15:8–10, 13–14, 17–30

⁸In the thirty-eighth year of Azariah king of Judah, Zechariah son of Jeroboam became king of Israel in Samaria, and he reigned six months. ⁹He did evil in the eyes of the Lord, as his fathers had done. He did not turn away from the sins of Jeroboam son of Nebat, which he had caused Israel to commit.

¹⁰Shallum son of Jabesh conspired against Zechariah. He attacked him in front of the people, assassinated him and succeeded him as king.

. . . .

¹³Shallum son of Jabesh became king in the thirty-ninth year of Uzziah king of Judah, and he reigned in Samaria one month. ¹⁴Then Menahem son of Gadi went from Tirzah up to Samaria. He attacked Shallum son of Jabesh in Samaria, assassinated him and succeeded him as king.

. . . .

¹⁷In the thirty-ninth year of Azariah king of Judah, Menahem son of Gadi became king of Israel, and he reigned in Samaria ten years. ¹⁸He did evil in the eyes of the Lord. During his entire reign he did not turn away from the sins of Jeroboam son of Nebat, which he had caused Israel to commit.

¹⁹Then Pul king of Assyria invaded the land, and Menahem gave him a thousand talents of silver to gain his support and strengthen his own hold on the kingdom. ²⁰Menahem exacted this money from Israel. Every

> wealthy man had to contribute fifty shekels of silver to be given to the king of Assyria. So the king of Assyria withdrew and stayed in the land no longer.
> ²¹As for the other events of Menahem's reign, and all he did, are they not written in the book of the annals of the kings of Israel? ²²Menahem rested with his fathers. And Pekahiah his son succeeded him as king.
> ²³In the fiftieth year of Azariah king of Judah, Pekahiah son of Menahem became king of Israel in Samaria, and he reigned two years. ²⁴Pekahiah did evil in the eyes of the Lord. He did not turn away from the sins of Jeroboam son of Nebat, which he had caused Israel to commit. ²⁵One of his chief officers, Pekah son of Remaliah, conspired against him. Taking fifty men of Gilead with him, he assassinated Pekahiah, along with Argob and Arieh, in the citadel of the royal palace at Samaria. So Pekah killed Pekahiah and succeeded him as king.
> ²⁶The other events of Pekahiah's reign, and all he did, are written in the book of the annals of the kings of Israel.
> ²⁷In the fifty-second year of Azariah king of Judah, Pekah son of Remaliah became king of Israel in Samaria, and he reigned twenty years. ²⁸He did evil in the eyes of the Lord. He did not turn away from the sins of Jeroboam son of Nebat, which he had caused Israel to commit.
> ²⁹In the time of Pekah king of Israel, Tiglath-Pileser king of Assyria came and took Ijon, Abel Beth Maacah, Janoah, Kedesh and Hazor. He took Gilead and Galilee, including all the land of Naphtali, and deported the people to Assyria. ³⁰Then Hoshea son of Elah conspired against Pekah son of Remaliah. He attacked and assassinated him, and then succeeded him as king in the twentieth year of Jotham son of Uzziah.

Eternal Optimism (14:23–29)

Jeroboam, a great-grandson of Jehu, became the king of Israel in 786 B.C. Biblical commentators have designated him as Jeroboam II to distinguish him from the previous Jeroboam who led the rebellion against Solomon's son Rehoboam and became the first king of the Northern kingdom of Israel (1 Kings 11—15).

The introduction of Jeroboam II follows the format the writer used in introducing the kings of Israel (2 Kings 14:23–24). It differed somewhat from the way he introduced kings of Judah. The one for Israel usually included the chronological link with a king from Judah, the length of reign, the name of the capital from which he ruled, and an evaluation of the king.

Every king of Israel received a negative evaluation in 1 and 2 Kings, and Jeroboam II was no exception (14:24). The thought was that the kingdom had come into existence in a rebellious way (against the dynasty of David). Thus, nothing positive or good could have resulted from an evil beginning. The demonstration of this principle was the fact that Jeroboam I established idolatrous centers of worship at Dan and Bethel to compete with Jerusalem. Since every successive king of Israel continued to support those worship places, they "did not turn away from the sins of Jeroboam son of Nebat" (14:24).

> *They neither provided positive leadership nor warned the Israelites of the danger of disobeying God.*

Jeroboam II ruled Israel from the capital city of Samaria (14:23). Omri and Ahab were responsible for establishing Samaria as the capital of Israel. It was near Shechem in the central hill country of Samaria and was well-fortified. It would serve as Israel's capital until Israel's defeat at the hand of the Assyrians.

Although Jeroboam II received the usual condemnation, the writer recognized that this king did some positive things. He credited Jeroboam with some military success (14:28) resulting in geographical expansion (14:25, 28). "Lebo Hamath" and "the Sea of Arabah" convey the idea that Jeroboam sought to restore the northern and eastern boundaries of the kingdom of David and Solomon. "Yaudi" (14:28) refers either to the Southern kingdom of Judah or to a small state in Syria.

The Assyrian Empire

From their homeland in northern Mesopotamia (along the Tigris River), the Assyrians enjoyed several periods of power and expansion from the fourteenth century to the late seventh century B.C. They engaged in military campaigns in order to expand their territorial claims, to gain and maintain control of major trade routes, and to secure raw materials not native to their land (timber, metals, etc.).

They sought to control territory nearest their homeland to ensure their security. Beyond that ring of protection, they exerted their control over the leaders of smaller nations through protection promised if those leaders paid an annual tribute to the Assyrian king. If the local leaders failed to do this, then the Assyrian army would conquer that land and carry out a population import/export policy. The aim of this policy was to break down nationalistic loyalty through the mixing of the various peoples.

The Assyrians were fierce warriors fighting in behalf of their god, Asshur, a national warrior god. They believed the whole earth was his rightful domain.

Jeroboam II enjoyed a long and quite prosperous reign in Israel (786–746 B.C.). The prophet Amos ministered in Israel during his reign. The words of Amos reveal that it was a time of economic prosperity. Amos constantly chided the wealthy people for taking advantage of the poor. The condemnation of Israel's religious and business practices by Amos reveals that she did not deserve this period of economic prosperity. These "good times" in Israel surely resulted from God's grace and goodness. Instead of recognizing that fact, Jeroboam and his subjects seemed to live in pious or false optimism. They refused to acknowledge their disobedience to God.

> *Jeroboam and his subjects seemed to live in pious or false optimism.*

Israel considered her prosperity to be sent from God due to a prophetic word (14:25). The mystery is that although "Jonah son of Amittai" is language identical to Jonah 1:1, the Book of Jonah contains no particular word related to geographical expansion of Israel. In fact it contains no divinely-sent word to Israel at all. It concerns a prophetic message for the Assyrians. As Amos declared, everybody did not share in the economic prosperity. God's awareness of the suffering (2 Kings 14:26) echoes Exodus 2:23–25, which describes God's concern for the slaves in Egypt.

Jeroboam II enjoyed a rather lengthy reign of peace and prosperity, but at his death everything changed. For her last decades of existence, Israel would never again experience these realities. The "book of the annals of the kings of Israel" (2 Kings 14:28) refers to the royal records kept by the scribes of the court.

Internal Deception (15:8–10, 13–14)

While Jeroboam II enjoyed a long and prosperous reign in Israel, Azariah (15:1–7; also called Uzziah, 15:13) had a similar experience as the king of Judah (783–742 B.C.). At the death of Jeroboam II, his son Zechariah became the king of Israel. He served in that position only six months (746–745 B.C.). He received the typical introduction and negative spiritual evaluation of the other kings of Israel. His reign was cut short by the palace intrigue led by Shallum, who was responsible for assassinating Zechariah. Zechariah was the last of the descendants of Jehu to sit on the

> *Leadership is an awesome responsibility.*

Lesson 9: Drifting Toward Disaster

Leadership Today

Think of someone you know personally, someone who has been a spiritual leader for you (past or present). It may be a pastor, staff minister, missions leader, Bible teacher, or deacon. Think of that person as you contemplate these questions:
- What was the key leadership quality of that leader?
- What made you admire or respect that leader?
- What made you want to follow the direction of that leader?
- Where did that leader lead you in your relationship with God?

throne of Israel (15:11–12). God fulfilled the word he had announced to Jehu (15:12; 10:30).

The rise to power by force had always been a route of choice in the Northern kingdom of Israel. Examples are plentiful, including Baasha (1 Kings 15:27–28); Zimri (1 Kings 16:10; Omri (1 Kings 16:15–20); and Jehu (2 Kings 9—10). The people of Israel were sadly accustomed to these murderous acts. Shallum conspired to bring about the death of the king of Israel "in front of the people" (15:10).

Violence began the brief reign of Shallum, and violence ended it after only one month. Menahem led a conspiracy against Shallum and assassinated him. Tirzah (15:14), six miles northeast of Shechem, was the capital of Israel prior to the construction of Samaria (1 Kings 14:17; 16:23–24). Shallum did not rule Israel even long enough to receive an evaluation. His brief rule did not matter. The Assyrian records were quite unkind to this king of Israel, calling him *the son of a nobody.*

> *Poor leaders abuse or manipulate others through the misuse of power and prestige, while good leaders exercise their authority wisely.*

A greedy lust for power is ugly in all of its expressions. It is ugly when it expresses itself (as here) through murderous violence. It is ugly when it expresses itself in church conflict through the deceptive telling of lies resulting in character assassination. It is also ugly when it is expressed through the manipulative abuse of others to get one's own way.

External Intervention (15:17–30)

Menahem (745–737 B.C.) was the only one of the last six kings of Israel to die a natural death (while still king). Under this king the kingdom of

1 AND 2 KINGS: *Leaders and Followers—Failed and Faithful*

Israel continued its patterned drift toward national disaster. As the reader has come to expect, the writer asserted that this king also failed to be a worthy leader of God's people. He did evil "during his entire reign" (2 Kings 15:18).

During Menahem's reign Israel encountered the intervention of an outside power (15:19–20). Biblical commentators have struggled to understand the difficult language of these verses and in fact have come to no consensus about what they mean. Menahem was either a victim of this intervention or possibly the one who was responsible for it.

The prevalent view is that the Assyrians invaded the land of Israel on their own initiative. After Assyria experienced a period of decline and weakness, Tiglath-Pileser III (745–727 B.C.) was the architect and founder of a resurgence of the Assyrian Empire. "Pul" (15:19) was a throne name he acquired after he defeated Babylon and the name the Old Testament often uses for him. It may be that Tiglath-Pileser III invaded Israel with the thought of territorial expansion in mind. As a result Menahem paid him tribute or protection money. This receiving of tribute (an annual cash "gift") was an important element in Assyrian expansion policy. Paying tribute money to the Assyrians meant that a nation recognized their authority or power over it. The alternative to paying tribute was to be conquered by the Assyrians and designated as one of their provinces. Between the two alternatives, Menahem chose the former.

> The phrase *servant leader* captures the two basic components of good leadership.

Some interpreters note that the Hebrew word rendered "invaded" (15:19) is the common word for coming into or entering a place and not the normal term used to describe military action. Could Menahem have invited Tiglath-Pileser III to bring an Assyrian presence to Israel because he was experiencing a challenge to his power by a rival? The closing words of verse 19 may support such a contention. In this scenario Menahem did not want to be overthrown or assassinated.

Whatever the rationale for the Assyrian presence, Menahem paid tribute to the Assyrians. In order to fulfill that obligation, he raised the taxes on his subjects (15:20). We do not have to speculate how popular a move that would have been. The paying of protection money successfully resolved the crisis.

When Menahem died, his son Pekahiah assumed the throne of Israel (15:23–26). His brief reign (737–736 B.C.) continued the drift toward disaster as he followed the pattern of his predecessors. He did that which was evil in the sight of God. Pekah, "one of his chief officers," was responsible for killing Pekahiah "in the citadel of the royal palace" (15:25). This death certainly resulted from an insider conspiracy or a palace coup.

Pekah would be the prime suspect if Menahem did indeed experience a rival claimant to the throne of Israel. The support for this insurgency might have come from the area east of the Jordan River or "Gilead" (15:25). Argob and Arieh are place names rather than personal names and evidently are related to Gilead.

Pekah (736–732 B.C.) received the customary royal introduction and negative evaluation (15:27–28). A reign of "twenty years" (15:27) presents difficult chronological problems when one attempts to reconcile this figure with the king list of Judah and with Assyrian inscriptions. Part of the solution may be that the writer meant to convey the time when Pekah first rebelled against the authority of Menahem and acted as if he himself were the king.

During Pekah's reign, the Assyrian ruler Tiglath-Pileser III again came to Israel (15:29). This visit was certainly an invasion. He conquered the territory north (Galilee) and east (Gilead) of the heartland of Israel. The displacement of populations was another characteristic of Assyrian imperial policy (15:29). The Assyrians attempted to mix the various ethnic groups in their empire to achieve the aim of reducing nationalistic loyalties that would compete with their designs for their empire.

> They refused to acknowledge their disobedience to God.

Implications and Actions

All the kings of Israel we examined in this study were poor examples of what God desires in leaders of his people. The kingdom of Israel paid a terrible price for their poor leadership. Leadership is an awesome responsibility. Poor leaders abuse or manipulate others through the misuse of power and prestige, while good leaders exercise their authority wisely.

The phrase *servant leader* captures the two basic components of good leadership. *Leader* emphasizes the guiding or influencing of others in a direction that honors or pleases God. *Servant* focuses on the attitudes of a good leader who understands that he or she leads under the direction of

God. In addition, this leader always has in mind the best interests of the followers and is willing to invest energy in their behalf.

Every group needs quality leadership. If it is lacking, then that group is drifting in a dangerous direction, away from the purpose and plan of God.

QUESTIONS

1. How would the reign of Jeroboam II be an example of the people of God being lulled to sleep by economic good times and failing to realize the deficiencies in their relationship to God?

2. Menahem may have invited the Assyrians (who would ultimately defeat Israel) to intervene in Israel's internal affairs. What are some things we invite into our lives that have the capability of destroying us?

3. What are the most important responsibilities of Christian leaders with regard to those who follow them? What are the most important responsibilities of Christian followers with regard to keeping their leaders accountable?

4. Most leaders will not resort to physical assassination as the kings of Israel did, but what are some ways modern leaders sometimes abuse or misuse their authority?

Focal Text
2 Kings 17:1–18, 21–23

Background
2 Kings 17

Main Idea
The people brought their destruction on themselves because of their unfaithfulness to God.

Question to Explore
Why do nations fail and pass away into the dust of history?

Study Aim
To lead the class to summarize why Israel was defeated and exiled, never to return, and to suggest ways to avoid a similar situation today

Study and Action Emphases
- Affirm the Bible as our authoritative guide for life and ministry
- Develop a growing, vibrant faith

LESSON TEN

Death of a Nation

Quick Read
The truth applies both to individuals and to groups of individuals (nations). Human sinfulness cannot result in anything other than destruction. God surely punishes sin.

1 AND 2 KINGS: *Leaders and Followers—Failed and Faithful*

Death is one of the topics we tend to avoid, but when it occurs, we report it. Newspapers contain obituaries or reports of deaths. Obituaries usually include the dates and places of birth and death, a listing of family members of the deceased, and information about a memorial service honoring the one who has died. So an obituary reports the facts surrounding death.

Another kind of report regarding death is an autopsy. While the obituary expresses the facts of a death, an autopsy is the examination to determine the cause or reason for that death. Most autopsies are performed by coroners or medical examiners to provide information required by a death certificate. A forensic autopsy seeks information that will assist authorities in a criminal investigation. Teaching hospitals perform clinical/academic autopsies for research that improves understanding of physical diseases.

Second Kings 17 records the death of a nation, the kingdom of Israel. In its reporting of the death of Israel, the end of its existence, this chapter gives both obituary and autopsy information. Verses 1–6 narrate the events of the final decade of Israel's life. It is not enough, however, for us to know simply that Israel lost her life. The writer wants the reader to know the cause of death or why it happened.

This chapter contains far more autopsy information than obituary information. In this chapter we see clearly that the biblical authors of historical material provided for us not just the events of history but also the theological interpretation of those events. The material that the Jews call *The Former Prophets* (Joshua, Judges, Samuel, Kings) communicates the purpose and plan of God for Israel in granting her a land in which to live and how Israel, as a result of her constant disobedience, forfeited her right to live in that land.

The autopsy report of 2 Kings 17 is quite clear. God brought about the death of the Northern kingdom of Israel as his judgment on the nation's constant rebellion against him. Two questions beg our attention. Would Israel's death serve as a warning to Judah? Could it serve as a warning to us as the people of God?

2 Kings 17:1–18, 21–23

1In the twelfth year of Ahaz king of Judah, Hoshea son of Elah became king of Israel in Samaria, and he reigned nine years. **2**He did evil in the eyes of the Lord, but not like the kings of Israel who preceded him.

³Shalmaneser king of Assyria came up to attack Hoshea, who had been Shalmaneser's vassal and had paid him tribute. ⁴But the king of Assyria discovered that Hoshea was a traitor, for he had sent envoys to So king of Egypt, and he no longer paid tribute to the king of Assyria, as he had done year by year. Therefore Shalmaneser seized him and put him in prison. ⁵The king of Assyria invaded the entire land, marched against Samaria and laid siege to it for three years. ⁶In the ninth year of Hoshea, the king of Assyria captured Samaria and deported the Israelites to Assyria. He settled them in Halah, in Gozan on the Habor River and in the towns of the Medes.

⁷All this took place because the Israelites had sinned against the Lord their God, who had brought them up out of Egypt from under the power of Pharaoh king of Egypt. They worshiped other gods ⁸and followed the practices of the nations the Lord had driven out before them, as well as the practices that the kings of Israel had introduced. ⁹The Israelites secretly did things against the Lord their God that were not right. From watchtower to fortified city they built themselves high places in all their towns. ¹⁰They set up sacred stones and Asherah poles on every high hill and under every spreading tree. ¹¹At every high place they burned incense, as the nations whom the Lord had driven out before them had done. They did wicked things that provoked the Lord to anger. ¹²They worshiped idols, though the Lord had said, "You shall not do this." ¹³The Lord warned Israel and Judah through all his prophets and seers: "Turn from your evil ways. Observe my commands and decrees, in accordance with the entire Law that I commanded your fathers to obey and that I delivered to you through my servants the prophets."

¹⁴But they would not listen and were as stiff-necked as their fathers, who did not trust in the Lord their God. ¹⁵They rejected his decrees and the covenant he had made with their fathers and the warnings he had given them. They followed worthless idols and themselves became worthless. They imitated the nations around them although the Lord had ordered them, "Do not do as they do," and they did the things the Lord had forbidden them to do.

¹⁶They forsook all the commands of the Lord their God and made for themselves two idols cast in the shape of calves, and an Asherah pole. They bowed down to all the starry hosts, and they worshiped Baal. ¹⁷They sacrificed their sons and daughters in the fire. They practiced divination and sorcery and sold themselves to do evil in the eyes of the Lord, provoking him to anger.

1 AND 2 KINGS: *Leaders and Followers—Failed and Faithful*

> ¹⁸So the LORD was very angry with Israel and removed them from his presence. Only the tribe of Judah was left . . .
>
> . . . .
>
> ²¹When he tore Israel away from the house of David, they made Jeroboam son of Nebat their king. Jeroboam enticed Israel away from following the LORD and caused them to commit a great sin. ²²The Israelites persisted in all the sins of Jeroboam and did not turn away from them ²³until the LORD removed them from his presence, as he had warned through all his servants the prophets. So the people of Israel were taken from their homeland into exile in Assyria, and they are still there.

Experiencing God's Judgment (17:1–6)

The final king of Israel was Hoshea (732–724 B.C.). It is more than a little ironic that one whose name means *Yahweh saves* was the king who felt the destruction of God's judgment. Equally stunning is that this king on whose watch the Israelites were taken from the land of Canaan into exile shared the same Hebrew name as the one under whose leadership the Israelites entered that land (Joshua).

Hoshea had become king by leading a conspiracy against his predecessor Pekah and assassinating him (2 Kings 15:30). Hoshea received the typical negative evaluation of all the kings of Israel (17:2). The absence of any word concerning religious unfaithfulness may be due to his preoccupation with the political crisis of his reign, the looming presence of the Assyrians.

The Assyrian king Shalmaneser V (727–722 B.C.) was the son and successor of the great Tiglath-Pileser III (15:19–20). Even as Menahem had paid tribute to the father, Hoshea paid tribute to the son (17:3). This action demonstrated that Hoshea recognized his subservient position to the Assyrians.

Each and every generation was sinful.

At some point Hoshea foolishly decided he would not send the tribute money to Shalmaneser. Knowing what that meant, he attempted to persuade the Egyptian king to help him in his resistance to the Assyrian king. "So" (17:4) is probably the Hebrew rendering of the Egyptian word *Sais*, the name of a place where the pharaoh lived. The reading would then be, *to So, to the king of Egypt*. During this period

The Fate of the Israelites

What happened to the people of the Northern kingdom (the Israelites)? The Assyrians deported some of them (2 Kings 17:6). It is probable that the Assyrian policy of moving people groups in order to break down ethnic purity and local loyalty was successful. They likely intermarried with other groups where they were resettled. As a result these Israelites were lost to history. This fact later produced fanciful theories of the fate of the "lost tribes of Israel."

As to the Israelites who remained in the land around Samaria, they too intermarried with groups that the Assyrians imported (2 Kings 17:24). Their descendants were called Samaritans. The Jews (remnant of the Southern kingdom of Judah) who returned from their own exile in Babylon did not allow the Samaritans any part in the rebuilding of Jerusalem (Ezra 4:1–3; see Nehemiah 4:7). When Jesus asked a woman for a drink from a well near Samaria, she was surprised and reminded him that "Jews do not associate with Samaritans" (John 4:9).

Egypt was no match for the superior Assyrian power. The prophet Hosea, who ministered to Israel during these critical years, repeatedly asserted that it was foolish to place any trust in the ability of Egypt to assist Israel (Hosea 5:13; 7:11; 12:1).

Shalmaneser considered the withholding of tribute and the appeal to Egypt as an act of rebellion. He responded predictably. The root of "traitor" (2 Kings 17:4) means *to bind* and was used occasionally to describe the ornamental bindings on clothing. The Assyrian king accused Hosea of seeking to be *bound* in loyalty to another king.

Note the order of events in these verses. Shalmaneser came to attack Hoshea (17:3), captured and confined him (17:4), and invaded the land of Israel (17:5). The royal power of Hoshea had ended. Shalmaneser "laid siege" to the capital city of Samaria for three years (17:5). The siege was a central part of Assyrian war strategy. They put a city under siege by surrounding it and cutting it off from any outside military assistance as well as from food supplies and water sources. Frequently residents would surrender only after a starvation crisis occurred. The length of this siege is testimony to the massive fortifications Omri and Ahab had constructed to protect Samaria.

> The Israelites sinned in the beginning and throughout their existence until God brought an end to their national life (17:23).

The Assyrian defeat of Israel is described in both the Old Testament and Assyrian records. The fall of Samaria occurred in 722 B.C., years of transition between Shalmaneser V (727–722 B.C.) and his brother Sargon II (722–705 B.C.). Sargon declared in his royal archives that he was responsible for the fall of Samaria.

The Assyrian Empire brought an end to the kingdom of Israel. The Assyrian records state that they deported 27,290 people from Israel (probably the number of men). We have already noted the population displacements that the Assyrians utilized in order to break down local, ethnic, and national loyalties. That goal is certainly reflected in the geographical diversity of these locations (17:6). Halah was in northern Mesopotamia, northeast of Nineveh. Gozan was a city state in far northwestern Mesopotamia (between Assyria and Syria). The territory of the Medes was in the Zagros Mountains east of Mesopotamia. While they moved some people out, they moved others into Israel, importing people from five different locations (17:24–41).

> *God can and does judge those who are unfaithful to him.*

Rejecting God's Direction (17:7–13)

The obituary is usually briefer than the autopsy work and report. Second Kings 17 is no exception. While the first six verses tell us that the kingdom of Israel came to an end through a military defeat at the hand of the Assyrians, verses 7–23 explain the reasons this death of a nation occurred. Ultimately it was Israel's God Yahweh and not the Assyrians who brought about the defeat of Israel. He punished them in this way as his judgment on their rejecting his direction. They "sinned" (17:7) against God, missing the goal or purpose of God for their national life.

> *God was fully justified in bringing judgment to Israel.*

The writer emphasized the gravity of the sins of Israel by placing them within their proper historical and religious context. These Israelites descended from the people whom Yahweh had delivered from Egyptian slavery. He chose them to be his people. He bound himself to them through a covenant relationship made at Sinai. The first of the Ten Commandments that summarized their covenantal responsibility

What Can We Do? Forum

As a community leader you are invited to participate as a panelist in a forum. The subject of the forum is "What Can We Do?" Panel members are asked to share their reactions and thoughts to the following scenario: Assume that attitudes and practices in our nation/culture are displeasing to God. As a result God has chosen to judge or punish us severely. What could we do, if anything, to avoid this judgment?

It is now your turn to speak. What would you say?

---

prohibited the recognition of any other god but Yahweh. Instead of obeying this word, they had "worshiped other gods" (17:7).

Two things contributed to this idolatrous worship of other gods. One was the temptation provided by the other people groups in the land of Canaan, most specifically the temptation to worship Baal, the fertility god of the Canaanites. At the same time, the royal leaders were accountable to God for their role in importing idolatrous practices or in developing their own (17:8). Israel's kings had proven to be unworthy leaders of God's people. It is unclear what the Israelites did "secretly" (17:9), for the various things mentioned in verses 9–11 were public worship practices.

> . . . Nations like individuals are accountable to God.

The land was dotted with numerous "high places." These sites on a hill or mountain served as a place where the people participated in the worship of the pagan god Baal. The "high places" generally had an altar as well as other furniture used in worship. Two of these items were "sacred stones," upright stones or pillars, and "Asherah poles," wooden objects that represented the goddess partner of El and mother of Baal. The burning of incense (along with the sacrifices) was practiced within both the legitimate worship of Israel and in many pagan forms of worship.

The Israelite sin of worshiping other gods stood in opposition to every way that God had revealed himself to Israel and communicated with them. Of course it violated the covenant agreement that they had made with Yahweh. They had violated both the first of the Ten Commandments (17:8) and also the second one, which prohibited use of physical images in worship (17:12). Their worship also rejected God's instructions that he gave them through "prophets and seers" (17:13). Hosea was one of these prophets who strongly urged Israel to repent of her sinful ways (Hosea 6:1–3; 14:1–3).

Note that the prophets warned both Israel and Judah. The question was whether the death of Israel would be an effective warning and preventive word keeping Judah from suffering the same fate. Only time would tell.

Provoking the Lord's Anger (17:14–18)

I am willing to give the ancient Israelites the benefit of the doubt. I do not believe they intentionally desired to anger God, but that was the consequence resulting from their sinful ways. The final generation of Israelites suffered the punishment sent by God through the Assysians. That does not mean, however, that they were the only sinful generation or the most sinful one. Each and every generation was sinful.

> They "sinned" (17:7) against God, missing the goal or purpose of God for their national life.

The "fathers" (17:14) denoted the generation with which God established the covenant at Sinai (17:15). Technically this generation was the first one of the people that God chose, delivered, and promised to give a land. "Stiff-necked" (17:14) refers literally to the back of one's neck. The sign of respect was the lifting up of the face to another, while the sign of disgust or disdain was to turn one's back to another. Even as that first generation of Israelites failed to trust God during their wilderness experience, other generations who followed them angered God.

In the same way the first generation of Israelites in the Northern kingdom was a sinful one. It was her first king Jeroboam I who built the two calf idols, placing them at Bethel and Dan, his southern and northern borders (1 Kings 12:25–30). These served as rivals to worship offered in Jerusalem.

While previously the writer listed some of the pagan places and worship objects (2 Kings 17:9–11), he now detailed some of the worship practices of the Israelites that the Lord had expressly forbidden them to engage in (17:16–17). They dabbled in astrology ("starry hosts") and fertility worship to seek the productivity of their flocks and fields ("Baal"). They demonstrated their lack of trust in God's guidance by preferring forbidden ways of seeking guidance from God rather than depending on the ways God made himself available to them (see Deuteronomy 18:9–22).

God chose these people called Israel to be a vehicle of revealing himself to the world. Instead they spent their energy in worshiping other gods and practicing prohibited ways. These idols were "worthless" (17:15). The root meaning of this word is *vapor* or *breath*, *vanity* or *emptiness*. Their devotion to gods who were themselves nothing caused the people to be less valuable in revealing God to others. This did indeed create anger within God (17:11, 17, 18).

The evidence of Israel's sinful rebellion was impressive. God was fully justified in bringing judgment to Israel. Although at this time the Southern kingdom of Judah did not suffer defeat as Israel did, she was guilty of the same unfaithfulness to God (17:19–20).

Earning God's Judgment (17:21–23)

These three verses provide an overview summary of the entire two hundred years of Israel's existence as a political entity (922–722 B.C.). The Northern kingdom began in part as a judgment of God. Yahweh was the "he" who "tore" Israel away from the Davidic dynasty and Rehoboam (17:21). This echoes the very language of the prophetic word delivered by Ahijah to Jeroboam I (1 Kings 11:31).

From the beginning, Jeroboam I led the Israelites into sin. Long after his death the nation continued in that same path (2 Kings 17:22). The Israelites sinned in the beginning and throughout their existence until God brought an end to their national life (17:23). The Assyrians relocated many of the Israelites, and they were still in those areas (17:6) when 2 Kings was written (about 560 B.C.).

Implications and Actions

We should be cautious in applying these kinds of biblical texts regarding God's relationship with Israel and Judah to our national experience in the United States. Although some would draw some historical similarities, we must remember the differences. First, God chose Israel to be his people as a part of his plan of providing salvation. God has not established a covenant relationship with our nation as he did with ancient Israel. Further, we are not ruled by a king whose purpose is to be God's ruling representative.

1 AND 2 KINGS: *Leaders and Followers—Failed and Faithful*

Having expressed caution in drawing specific parallels, let me also say that nations like individuals are accountable to God. God can and does judge those who are unfaithful to him. The study today is about the people of God called Israel. It seems to me that the most direct relevance and application is to the people of God called Christian.

Tragically Christians are having less and less of an influential impact on our larger culture. What can we do? Our responsibility as followers of Christ is to participate in furthering God's mission through conversion of individuals to Christ. May God give us power and courage for the task.

QUESTIONS

1. What does Israel's history teach us about the importance of each generation's faithfulness to God?

2. What are some of the ways today that we (individuals, churches, nations) reject God's guidance and direction?

3. Do you agree or disagree with the writer's idea of showing caution in the direct application of Israel's responsibility to God with that of the United States? Explain why you agree or disagree.

4. How do you seek to reconcile an understanding of the sovereignty of God over all nations with the presence of cruel national leaders who oppress their people?

5. Israel lost her opportunity to be God's servant because of her unfaithfulness. What kind of opportunities for service to God might we forfeit if we fail to be faithful?

Missing the Last Chance: The Sequel

UNIT FIVE

2 Kings 18–25

The people of God in Israel experienced the complete judgment of God as the Northern kingdom came to an end in 722 B.C. Would the Southern kingdom of Judah learn anything from the experience of their kinspeople? The short answer is *no*. Even so, Judah would not experience the judgment of God until about 135 years later.

It is possible that the reason for such a delay in God's outpouring of judgment on Judah was due to the spiritual times of renewal that Judah experienced under the leadership of two of her greatest kings, Hezekiah and Josiah. These two kings were associated with two of the greatest of the Old Testament prophets, Isaiah and Jeremiah, respectively.

These two kings were the best examples in the Southern kingdom of what the king as God's earthly representative should be. This reality should remind us that even when God's judgment seems to be inevitable, it is possible for the people of God to have a positive influence.

In spite of the faithfulness to God of these two kings, the Babylonians ultimately ended the existence of the kingdom of Judah. This defeat of Judah and the destruction of Jerusalem were absolutely devastating to the chosen people of God. God himself had chosen to dwell especially in Jerusalem, in the temple. God had granted to Israel a promise that the royal family of David would forever rule over God's throne (2 Samuel 7). These convictions became the basis for their understanding that Zion (the temple mount) would never be defeated, for God himself would defend it. How could Judah, Jerusalem, and the Davidic king be defeated?

The answer, of course, is that God engineered this defeat by a foreign oppressor. It was God's judgment on their disobedience. In 586 B.C. Judah received a judgment similar to that of the Northern kingdom of Israel. It was the most devastating experience of the people of God that occurred during the entire period of the Old Testament.[1]

UNIT FIVE. MISSING THE LAST CHANCE: THE SEQUEL (2 KINGS 18—25)

Lesson 11	When the Situation Is Desperate	2 Kings 18:1–19, 29–31; 19:1–11, 14–20
Lesson 12	The Only Hope	2 Kings 22:1—23:4
Lesson 13	The Bitter End	2 Kings 23:31–32, 36–37; 24:8–9, 18–20; 25:8–21

NOTES

1. Unless otherwise indicated, all Scripture quotations in unit five are from the New International Version.

Focal Text
2 Kings 18:1–19, 29–31; 19:1–11, 14–20

Background
2 Kings 18—19

Main Idea
People who are faithful to God can trust God to care for their needs.

Question to Explore
When the situation is desperate, can God be trusted to help?

Study Aim
To summarize the meaning of the story of Hezekiah's challenge by the Assyrians and to respond with trust in God in areas of life where I face challenges

Study and Action Emphases
- Affirm the Bible as our authoritative guide for life and ministry
- Develop a growing, vibrant faith
- Equip people for servant leadership

LESSON ELEVEN
When the Situation Is Desperate

Quick Read
We have two choices when we face difficulties. Either we can attempt to deal with the circumstance completely on our own, or we can trust God to care for us.

1 AND 2 KINGS: *Leaders and Followers—Failed and Faithful*

It was a beautiful day in April of 2003, one perfectly suited for mountain climbing. Aron Ralston, a twenty-seven-year-old from Aspen, Colorado, planned to spend his Saturday climbing in the Blue John Canyon area of southeastern Utah. He was preparing for a later trip to the Denali National Park in Alaska.

The day turned tragic when, as a result of a rock slide, his right arm was trapped by an 800-pound boulder. He could not pry himself loose. On the third day he ran out of food and water. He was in a desperate situation. On the fifth day he made a critical decision. Using his pocket knife he cut through flesh and blood vessels, and he snapped the bones in his right forearm. In just over an hour he severed his right arm below the elbow and escaped a certain death.

He applied a tourniquet to his arm to stop the bleeding and rappelled some sixty-five feet down the face of the canyon. After walking for six miles, he met two hikers who helped him find medical assistance. His book *Between a Rock and a Hard Place* recounts his frightening ordeal and courageous recovery.[1]

Aron Ralston found himself in a desperate situation and took an extreme action. Hezekiah was one of the kings of Judah who also found himself in a desperate situation. He also took an extreme action. He trusted in Yahweh, the God of Israel and Judah, and God took care of his needs.

2 Kings 18:1–19, 29–31

¹In the third year of Hoshea son of Elah king of Israel, Hezekiah son of Ahaz king of Judah began to reign. ²He was twenty-five years old when he became king, and he reigned in Jerusalem twenty-nine years. His mother's name was Abijah daughter of Zechariah. ³He did what was right in the eyes of the LORD, just as his father David had done. ⁴He removed the high places, smashed the sacred stones and cut down the Asherah poles. He broke into pieces the bronze snake Moses had made, for up to that time the Israelites had been burning incense to it. (It was called Nehushtan.)
⁵Hezekiah trusted in the LORD, the God of Israel. There was no one like him among all the kings of Judah, either before him or after him. ⁶He held fast to the LORD and did not cease to follow him; he kept the commands the LORD had given Moses. ⁷And the LORD was with him; he was successful in whatever he undertook. He rebelled against the

Lesson 11: When the Situation Is Desperate

king of Assyria and did not serve him. ⁸From watchtower to fortified city, he defeated the Philistines, as far as Gaza and its territory.

⁹In King Hezekiah's fourth year, which was the seventh year of Hoshea son of Elah king of Israel, Shalmaneser king of Assyria marched against Samaria and laid siege to it. ¹⁰At the end of three years the Assyrians took it. So Samaria was captured in Hezekiah's sixth year, which was the ninth year of Hoshea king of Israel. ¹¹The king of Assyria deported Israel to Assyria and settled them in Halah, in Gozan on the Habor River and in towns of the Medes. ¹²This happened because they had not obeyed the LORD their God, but had violated his covenant—all that Moses the servant of the LORD commanded. They neither listened to the commands nor carried them out.

¹³In the fourteenth year of King Hezekiah's reign, Sennacherib king of Assyria attacked all the fortified cities of Judah and captured them. ¹⁴So Hezekiah king of Judah sent this message to the king of Assyria at Lachish: "I have done wrong. Withdraw from me, and I will pay whatever you demand of me." The king of Assyria exacted from Hezekiah king of Judah three hundred talents of silver and thirty talents of gold. ¹⁵So Hezekiah gave him all the silver that was found in the temple of the LORD and in the treasuries of the royal palace.

¹⁶At this time Hezekiah king of Judah stripped off the gold with which he had covered the doors and doorposts of the temple of the LORD, and gave it to the king of Assyria.

¹⁷The king of Assyria sent his supreme commander, his chief officer and his field commander with a large army, from Lachish to King Hezekiah at Jerusalem. They came up to Jerusalem and stopped at the aqueduct of the Upper Pool, on the road to the Washerman's Field. ¹⁸They called for the king; and Eliakim son of Hilkiah the palace administrator, Shebna the secretary, and Joah son of Asaph the recorder went out to them.

¹⁹The field commander said to them, "Tell Hezekiah: "'This is what the great king, the king of Assyria, says: On what are you basing this confidence of yours?

. . . .

²⁹This is what the king says: Do not let Hezekiah deceive you. He cannot deliver you from my hand. ³⁰Do not let Hezekiah persuade you to trust in the LORD when he says, 'The LORD will surely deliver us; this city will not be given into the hand of the king of Assyria.'

³¹"Do not listen to Hezekiah. This is what the king of Assyria says: Make peace with me and come out to me. Then every one of you will eat from his own vine and fig tree and drink water from his own cistern. . . .

1 AND **2** KINGS: *Leaders and Followers—Failed and Faithful*

2 Kings 19:1–11, 14–20

¹When King Hezekiah heard this, he tore his clothes and put on sackcloth and went into the temple of the LORD. ²He sent Eliakim the palace administrator, Shebna the secretary and the leading priests, all wearing sackcloth, to the prophet Isaiah son of Amoz. ³They told him, "This is what Hezekiah says: This day is a day of distress and rebuke and disgrace, as when children come to the point of birth and there is no strength to deliver them. ⁴It may be that the LORD your God will hear all the words of the field commander, whom his master, the king of Assyria, has sent to ridicule the living God, and that he will rebuke him for the words the LORD your God has heard. Therefore pray for the remnant that still survives."

⁵When King Hezekiah's officials came to Isaiah, ⁶Isaiah said to them, "Tell your master, 'This is what the LORD says: Do not be afraid of what you have heard—those words with which the underlings of the king of Assyria have blasphemed me. ⁷Listen! I am going to put such a spirit in him that when he hears a certain report, he will return to his own country, and there I will have him cut down with the sword.'"

⁸When the field commander heard that the king of Assyria had left Lachish, he withdrew and found the king fighting against Libnah.

⁹Now Sennacherib received a report that Tirhakah, the Cushite king [of Egypt], was marching out to fight against him. So he again sent messengers to Hezekiah with this word: ¹⁰"Say to Hezekiah king of Judah: Do not let the god you depend on deceive you when he says, 'Jerusalem will not be handed over to the king of Assyria.' ¹¹Surely you have heard what the kings of Assyria have done to all the countries, destroying them completely. And will you be delivered?

. . . .

¹⁴Hezekiah received the letter from the messengers and read it. Then he went up to the temple of the LORD and spread it out before the LORD. ¹⁵And Hezekiah prayed to the LORD: "O LORD, God of Israel, enthroned between the cherubim, you alone are God over all the kingdoms of the earth. You have made heaven and earth. ¹⁶Give ear, O LORD, and hear; open your eyes, O LORD, and see; listen to the words Sennacherib has sent to insult the living God.

¹⁷"It is true, O LORD, that the Assyrian kings have laid waste these nations and their lands. ¹⁸They have thrown their gods into the fire and destroyed them, for they were not gods but only wood and stone, fashioned by men's hands. ¹⁹Now, O LORD our God, deliver us from his hand, so that all kingdoms on earth may know that you alone, O LORD, are God."

> **20**Then Isaiah son of Amoz sent a message to Hezekiah: "This is what the LORD, the God of Israel, says: I have heard your prayer concerning Sennacherib king of Assyria.

Trust in God Practiced (18:1–8)

King Hezekiah received considerable attention in the biblical material. We learn about him in the prophetic history (2 Kings 18—20), the prophetic material that repeats it almost verbatim (Isaiah 36—39), and the priestly history (2 Chronicles 29—32).

The introductions for the kings of Judah in 1 and 2 Kings include the chronological link with the king of Israel, the age of the king, and length of his reign. For most of them the writer also included the name of the queen mother. The king then received an evaluation, most of them negative in nature.

Hezekiah ruled Judah from 715 to 687/686 B.C. Since Hoshea's rule over Israel is dated as 732–724 B.C., verse 1 may have used Hezekiah's years of co-rule with his father Ahaz (735–715 B.C.). If that is not the case, we do not have the necessary information to resolve the differences.

Hezekiah was one of only two kings of Judah who received unqualified praise in this book (2 Kings 18:3). (Josiah, whom we will study in the next lesson, is the other.) Being compared favorably to David was the highest compliment. Hezekiah "trusted in the LORD" (18:5). The writer never used the Hebrew verb translated "trusted" (*batach*) to describe the attitude of any other king in this book, but he used this word for Hezekiah repeatedly (nine times in 2 Kings 18—19).

Hezekiah demonstrated this trust through his actions. His father Ahaz (16:1–3) was guilty of supporting the Baal fertility cult and importing the worship of the Assyrians. Hezekiah sought to destroy the things that were associated with pagan worship (18:4). See the comments on 2 Kings 17:9–11 in the previous lesson for the explanation of these idolatrous furnishings.

Hezekiah's religious reformation also included the destruction of the "bronze snake" (18:4). "Nehushtan" is a word found only here in the Old Testament and was probably a nickname. Moses constructed it for a positive purpose (Numbers 21:1–9), but later generations evidently used it in a negative way. The language "broke into pieces" denoted beating or melting the metal down into something else. The Chronicler (2 Chronicles 29—32) adds that Hezekiah did some repairs to the temple structure, offered extensive sacrifices of dedication, and led in the celebration of a special Passover. God honored Hezekiah's faithfulness to the covenant obligations by blessing him or granting him success (2 Kings 18:7).

Hezekiah also implemented political reforms or more accurately political expansion. He exerted his authority in the southwestern coastal area of Canaan, the ancestral land of the Philistines. These bold steps collided with the aims of Assyrian power in the region. His father Ahaz had paid tribute to Tiglath-Pileser III. It is possible that Hezekiah began to withhold tribute from the Assyrians (as Hoshea in Israel had done; see lesson ten on 2 Kings 17).

> *As we face desperate situations, we should trust God to be with us.*

Trust in God Tested (18:9–19, 29–31)

Hezekiah's steps of rebellion against the Assyrian Empire provided a test for his trust in Yahweh. Would he continue to trust in God? Verses 9–12 summarize the events narrated by 2 Kings 17:1–23 regarding the fall of Samaria and the reasons it occurred.

The Assyrian king Sennacherib (705–681 B.C.) attacked Judah when Hezekiah rebelled. This military action occurred in 701 B.C. It is mentioned in both the Old Testament and Assyrian records and depicted in sculpted scenes on the palace walls of Sennacherib at Nineveh.

The Assyrian king boasted that he captured or destroyed no less than forty-six towns and villages of Judah. These were fortified towns in the foothills that protected the four entrances from the coast into the Judean hills. Sennacherib established his headquarters at Lachish (18:14), a town in Judah, the town depicted most prominently in the sculpture on his palace walls.

> *Hezekiah had a strong trust in God and is a good role model for us in this area.*

Hezekiah was somewhat intimidated by the Assyrian show of force. "Done wrong" (18:14) is the common Hebrew word for missing the mark or a sinful act. He determined to bribe Sennacherib through offering gifts of precious metal. In order to fulfill his commitment, he gave the Assyrian ruler ornamental gold and silver from both the royal palace and the temple (18:15–16).

Introductory Formulas

Biblical scholarship uses the term "introductory formulas" to describe the phrases that introduce many of the prophetic speeches or sermons found in the Old Testament.

- The messenger formula *(This is what the Lord says)* is adapted from the words used by heralds or messengers who carried a message from the king to the various parts of his realm. The prophets declared the message of Yahweh the great King.
- The proclamation formula *(Hear the word of the Lord)* was the language of the priests when they prepared the people to receive an instructive word of Yahweh through the teaching of the law.
- The lawsuit formula *(The Lord has this against you)* came from the world of the justice system. In this way the prophets brought God's accusations of rebellion and waywardness against his people.
- The lament formula *(Woe to you)* utilized the words of sadness expressed by mourners over the loss of a family member or friend.

The gifts must not have impressed Sennacherib, for he initiated a diplomatic exchange with Hezekiah (18:17–18). The Assyrian spokesman recognized that it was a matter of trust. His king was curious as to the basis of Hezekiah's faith. The Hebrew word for trust occurs twice in verse 19 and five more times in verses 20–28.

The Assyrian spokesman felt that Hezekiah foolishly trusted in God, and he did not want Hezekiah to "deceive" others into sharing his strong belief (18:29). He asserted that Hezekiah (implied is "nor his God") could not deliver them from the hand of the powerful Assyrians. Trust in the Assyrians alone could bring them security and continued productivity (18:31). No country or its god had been successful in resisting the Assyrians (18:33–35). Hezekiah's servants reported this message to their king (18:37).

Trust in God Demonstrated (19:1–11)

Upon receiving the report, Hezekiah expressed his humility and sadness by wearing coarse clothing associated with the poor (19:1). The fact that he went to the temple in Jerusalem, appealed to a prophet, and included priests in the entourage signified that this was a spiritual crisis and not just a political one (19:2). Prophets frequently functioned in an intercessory role.

Usually the prophet confronted the king without an invitation, while here the king appealed to the prophet to give him a word of divine assurance. First, Hezekiah communicated an honest assessment of the desperate situation Judah faced (19:3). "Distress" denotes being in a cramped, narrow, tight, or restricted place. The root meaning of "rebuke" was to prove that something was right or to convince others, while "disgrace" signified something or someone who was in contempt toward God.

> We either believe or trust in the work of God, or we fail to believe him.

Second, Hezekiah wanted Isaiah's (and Yahweh's) assistance in this tight circumstance. He asked Isaiah to take this desperate situation to God in prayer. The term "remnant" (19:4) or *remaining portion* demonstrates how much suffering Judah had experienced already.

Isaiah took the matter to God and responded to Hezekiah's request with a word from God. Isaiah began with the words of the messenger formula, "This is what the Lord says" (19:6). The prophets routinely used it as they spoke words from the Great King to his earthly representative. Isaiah offered a word of strong reassurance. God would honor Hezekiah's trust in him. Isaiah encouraged the king not to be afraid. The command not to fear was due to the intervening work of God (19:7). Isaiah asserted that Sennacherib would not only retreat from his advance toward Jerusalem but also ultimately would die violently.

The writer does not convey to us whether Isaiah's word to Hezekiah was delivered to the representatives of Sennacherib. At the least the representatives understood that the king of Judah was not going to surrender to their master. Sennacherib's move from Lachish to Libnah was a move bringing him closer to Jerusalem (19:8). The Assyrian king was then distracted by a force advancing from Egypt. He sent messengers to tell Hezekiah that he would first deal with the Egyptians and then would return and finish off the Judeans. He declared that no religious opponent (19:10) or political opponent (19:11) had ever successfully repelled the Assyrians. "Depend" (19:10) is again the word that means *trust*, an attitude demonstrated by Hezekiah.

> The evidence of whether we trust God or not is the way we live our lives.

Trust in God Honored (19:14–20)

Not satisfied with oral negotiations, Sennacherib sent a written warning to Hezekiah (19:14). It reminded Hezekiah of many other countries that had resisted the Assyrians and no longer existed (19:10–13). The implication was that Hezekiah would simply be the next one in a long list of Assyria's conquered enemies. Sennacherib bragged in his royal archives that he surrounded Jerusalem and had Hezekiah confined "like a bird in a cage."

In a desperate situation Hezekiah took extreme measures. The king went to the temple himself to pray to Yahweh. First he affirmed the greatness of God (19:15). He praised Yahweh for being the Creator and the Sovereign over all the earth. "Enthroned between the cherubim" (19:15) referred to the area within the most holy place of the temple just above the lid of the ark of the covenant upon which the two angelic representations (cherubim) looked. Hezekiah may have stood as close to that place as he could when he offered this prayer.

When we are practicing (demonstrating) our faith in Christ, we should not be surprised if our faith is tested.

Hezekiah explained the present crisis to his great God (19:16–18). Of course he did not give God information God did not have. The explanation of circumstances allowed Hezekiah to reveal that he understood accurately this situation. He petitioned Yahweh because the threats of Sennacherib concerned not only the security of Hezekiah but also the reputation of Hezekiah's God. Indeed the Assyrians had defeated other peoples whose gods were not able to save them, but those gods were no match for Yahweh the living God.

Hezekiah then was specific in his request (19:19). He pleaded for God to deliver him and Judah from the menacing threats of the Assyrian king. Hezekiah asked God to deliver *us* so that others might know *you* or that others might come to realize that Yahweh alone was God.

Having faith does not mean that one will live an obstacle-free existence.

Isaiah again served in the mediator role and conveyed Yahweh's response to the king (19:20). Maybe Isaiah accompanied the king to the temple, and they both offered their petitions to God.

Isaiah boldly declared that the Assyrian king would not enter the city of Jerusalem but would withdraw and return to Nineveh (19:21–34). God honored Hezekiah's trust in him and imposed his will on this situation, whereupon the Assyrian king returned home (19:35–36). Eventually Sennacherib died violently at the hands of his own children in a palace revolt (19:37), even as Isaiah had proclaimed (19:6–7).

Hezekiah was one of the two best kings of Judah. When he faced desperate situations, he trusted in Yahweh. He was not perfect in his trust, however. At times he expressed quite selfish attitudes. A prime example is when Isaiah declared to him that God would ultimately punish Judah through the Babylonians, and Hezekiah was okay with that because it would not happen on his watch (20:12–29). The punishment of God was delayed but not completely avoided.

Implications and Actions

Hezekiah had a strong trust in God and is a good role model for us in this area. We either believe or trust in the work of God, or we fail to believe him. The evidence of whether we trust God or not is the way we live our lives. Remember the often repeated saying about proof and pudding. We show our trust in God by practicing our faith in the same way that doctors "practice" medicine and attorneys "practice" law. We do what God has taught us to do.

God will honor our faith in him.

When we are practicing (demonstrating) our faith in Christ, we should not be surprised if our faith is tested. Having faith does not mean that one will live an obstacle-free existence. Tests of our faith give us an opportunity to prove the sincerity or genuineness of our love for Jesus and our faith in him.

God will honor our faith in him. As we face desperate situations, we should trust God to be with us. He will not only be our companion during tough times, but he will also take care of our needs. God will strengthen our faith and trust through the tough times.

QUESTIONS

1. The lesson comments state that Hezekiah's trusting in God was an "extreme" action. What do you think is meant by that? Do you agree or disagree?

2. See James 2:14–26. What relevance, if any, do the thoughts in those verses have for Hezekiah's practice of his faith in God (2 Kings 18:3–8)?

3. Think of the most recent experience in your life that in some way tested your faith in Christ. What did you learn or gain from the experience?

NOTES

1. Aron Ralston, *Between a Rock and a Hard Place* (New York: Atria Books, 2004).

Focal Text
2 Kings 22:1—23:4

Background
2 Kings 22:1—23:30

Main Idea
Our only hope is to turn in faith to God and live in faithfulness to him.

Question to Explore
To whom shall we turn except to God, committing ourselves to live in faithfulness to him?

Study Aim
To describe the response of Josiah to the book of the law and to decide to commit or re-commit myself to live in faithfulness to God

Study and Action Emphases
- Affirm the Bible as our authoritative guide for life and ministry
- Share the gospel with all people
- Develop a growing, vibrant faith

LESSON TWELVE

The Only Hope

Quick Read
Being faithful to God is not simply one of several good foundations for life. God is the only true hope for our salvation.

1 AND 2 KINGS: *Leaders and Followers—Failed and Faithful*

No baseball fan would have considered him their best or only hope. William grew up in West Virginia and Ohio and was a good baseball player, especially with his glove. In fact, during his seventeen-year major league career, he earned the nickname "The Glove" for his fielding skills at second base. However, he was only an average hitter at the plate (.260), hitting only 138 career home runs (averaging 8 per year). He usually batted in the eighth position, just before the pitcher.

His Pittsburgh Pirates faced the mighty New York Yankees in the 1960 World Series. The Yankee lineup included the legendary names of Mantle, Maris, Berra, Bobby Richardson, and others. The Yankees had flexed their muscles, winning three games by scores of 16–3, 12–0, and 10–0. They played the deciding Game 7 on October 14, 1960, at Forbes Field in Pittsburgh.

None of those 36,683 fans would have considered him to be their best or only hope, but he did something nobody expected. He led off the bottom of the ninth inning with a blast that cleared the left field wall. As I write these lines, it is still the only walk-off homer (a home run in a team's last at-bat that ends the game immediately) in World Series Game 7 history. Although his Yankee counterpart at second base, Bobby Richardson, was named the Most Valuable Player of the World Series, Bill Mazeroski was not only Pittsburgh's best hope. He was their best hero, leading the Pirates to their first world championship in more than thirty years.

Josiah was a mere boy when he was anointed as the king of Judah. Nobody would have considered him their best hope to bring about a stirring religious reformation. Even so, he was not only their best hope for such a reality, but he became their best hero in leading the people in Judah in a recommitment of their desire to be faithful to God. This study is based on the two chapters in the prophetic history about Josiah (2 Kings 22—23).[1]

2 Kings 22:1-20

¹Josiah was eight years old when he became king, and he reigned in Jerusalem thirty-one years. His mother's name was Jedidah daughter of Adaiah; she was from Bozkath. ²He did what was right in the eyes of the LORD and walked in all the ways of his father David, not turning aside to the right or to the left.
³In the eighteenth year of his reign, King Josiah sent the secretary, Shaphan son of Azaliah, the son of Meshullam, to the temple of the LORD. He said: ⁴"Go up to Hilkiah the high priest and have him get ready the

money that has been brought into the temple of the Lord, which the doorkeepers have collected from the people. ⁵Have them entrust it to the men appointed to supervise the work on the temple. And have these men pay the workers who repair the temple of the Lord— ⁶the carpenters, the builders and the masons. Also have them purchase timber and dressed stone to repair the temple. ⁷But they need not account for the money entrusted to them, because they are acting faithfully."

⁸Hilkiah the high priest said to Shaphan the secretary, "I have found the Book of the Law in the temple of the Lord." He gave it to Shaphan, who read it. ⁹Then Shaphan the secretary went to the king and reported to him: "Your officials have paid out the money that was in the temple of the Lord and have entrusted it to the workers and supervisors at the temple." ¹⁰Then Shaphan the secretary informed the king, "Hilkiah the priest has given me a book." And Shaphan read from it in the presence of the king.

¹¹When the king heard the words of the Book of the Law, he tore his robes. ¹²He gave these orders to Hilkiah the priest, Ahikam son of Shaphan, Acbor son of Micaiah, Shaphan the secretary and Asaiah the king's attendant: ¹³"Go and inquire of the Lord for me and for the people and for all Judah about what is written in this book that has been found. Great is the Lord's anger that burns against us because our fathers have not obeyed the words of this book; they have not acted in accordance with all that is written there concerning us."

¹⁴Hilkiah the priest, Ahikam, Acbor, Shaphan and Asaiah went to speak to the prophetess Huldah, who was the wife of Shallum son of Tikvah, the son of Harhas, keeper of the wardrobe. She lived in Jerusalem, in the Second District. ¹⁵She said to them, "This is what the Lord, the God of Israel, says: Tell the man who sent you to me, ¹⁶'This is what the Lord says: I am going to bring disaster on this place and its people, according to everything written in the book the king of Judah has read. ¹⁷Because they have forsaken me and burned incense to other gods and provoked me to anger by all the idols their hands have made, my anger will burn against this place and will not be quenched.' ¹⁸Tell the king of Judah, who sent you to inquire of the Lord, 'This is what the Lord, the God of Israel, says concerning the words you heard: ¹⁹Because your heart was responsive and you humbled yourself before the Lord when you heard what I have spoken against this place and its people, that they would become accursed and laid waste, and because you tore your robes and wept in my presence, I have heard you, declares the Lord. ²⁰Therefore I will gather you to your fathers, and you will be buried in peace. Your eyes will not see all the disaster I am going to bring on this place.'"

So they took her answer back to the king.

> ## 2 Kings 23:1–4
>
> ¹Then the king called together all the elders of Judah and Jerusalem. ²He went up to the temple of the Lord with the men of Judah, the people of Jerusalem, the priests and the prophets—all the people from the least to the greatest. He read in their hearing all the words of the Book of the Covenant, which had been found in the temple of the Lord. ³The king stood by the pillar and renewed the covenant in the presence of the Lord—to follow the Lord and keep his commands, regulations and decrees with all his heart and all his soul, thus confirming the words of the covenant written in this book. Then all the people pledged themselves to the covenant.
>
> ⁴The king ordered Hilkiah the high priest, the priests next in rank and the doorkeepers to remove from the temple of the Lord all the articles made for Baal and Asherah and all the starry hosts. He burned them outside Jerusalem in the fields of the Kidron Valley and took the ashes to Bethel.

Repairing the House of God (22:1–7)

The introduction of the rule of Josiah (640–609 B.C.) includes all of the usual elements of the material regarding the kings of Judah. His mother's ancestral home, "Bozkath" (2 Kings 22:1), was in the foothills southwest of Jerusalem between Lachish and Eglon.

Josiah received the highest commendation found in this book (22:2). The writer declared three things about Josiah. First, Josiah's life was pleasing to the Lord. Second, he acted in the same way as his ancestor the great King David had. Third, Josiah followed the directions of Moses in "not turning aside to the right or left" (22:3; see Deuteronomy 5:32; 17:11). The writer of 2 Kings believed Josiah was an excellent example of the pattern for a good king found in Deuteronomy 17:14–20.

The extensive religious reformation inspired by Josiah began with the renovation of the temple (2 Kings 22:3–7). Evidently the worship place had been neglected during the long reign of Josiah's grandfather, the wicked king Manasseh (687/6–642 B.C.). In 2 Chronicles we learn that Josiah desired to strengthen his relationship to God in the eighth year of his reign and ordered a destruction of idolatrous places and practices four years later (2 Chronicles 34:3–7). Having destroyed competitors to it, he decided "in the eighteenth year" (2 Kings 22:3) to restore the beauty and dignity of the central worship place, the temple in Jerusalem.

The beginning of Josiah's destruction of pagan worship places in the twelfth year of his reign (628 B.C.) coincided with the ending days of the rule of the powerful Assyrian king Assurbanipal (668–627 B.C.). From the time of their king's death, the Assyrians were distracted by, challenged by, and ultimately defeated by the Babylonians. This period of relative Assyrian weakness allowed Josiah to accomplish his goals.

> *No time of renewal of the people of God has ever occurred apart from a deep sense of conviction of sin and a desire to confess that sinfulness to God and receive his forgiveness.*

The repair work involved cooperation between the palace (Shaphan) and the priests at the temple (Hilkiah). The planning described here (22:4–6) is the same preparation work necessary for construction projects today. In our language, they secured the financing, selected a general contractor, and delivered advance money to the sub-contractors, enabling them to purchase physical materials. While we can commend the high trust level demonstrated in verse 7, we realize that providing a full accounting of the receiving and spending of the resources of God's people is important.

Rediscovering the Law of God (22:8–13)

Let's say you make the decision to expand your current living space instead of moving to a larger house. As you begin the process of moving stuff out of a closet, you find boxes containing bundles of letters you had written to each other before you were married. You had almost forgotten the letters existed. The cleaning-out task is delayed while the two of you sit on the floor together reading your rediscovered thoughts.

The workers who were renovating the temple found a scroll and gave it to the priest Hilkiah. Its designation as "the Book of the Law" (22:8) denotes that it contained *Torah* or instruction from God. Of course the modern reader is curious as to why it was lost in the first place and needed to be rediscovered. Interpreters suggest that during the long and evil reign of Manasseh, it was either neglected and ignored or intentionally hidden to preserve it from being destroyed.

The other matter of curiosity has to do with its content. The writer does not reveal that to us. The best clue as to the content of this book can be seen in the actions Josiah took when he learned of its existence. These actions are strikingly similar to the themes and emphases of the Book of Deuteronomy. Many Old Testament interpreters since the time of Jerome (fourth century A.D.) have believed that there is a vital connection between the Book of Deuteronomy and the reformation of Josiah.

Realizing the significance of the scroll, Hilkiah delivered it to Shaphan in the king's palace. Shaphan read it himself and then read it to King Josiah (see 22:9–10).

Josiah made a threefold response when he heard the content of the scroll. First, he "tore his robes" (22:11), a symbolic act expressing his sadness and humility. It was not just a sorrow for knowing what the scroll said. It was a sorrow from the realization of the sinfulness of the people of Judah (22:13b). Second, the scroll produced a sincere conviction within the king. Third, as a result he determined to find out what he should do in leading the people to turn away from their unfaithfulness (22:12–13a).

> *Like Josiah we should be determined to make a difference.*

Josiah ordered his servants to find out how they could repent or turn to God. "Inquire" (22:13) is a technical term that signified the seeking of instruction or direction from God, usually from a priest at a sanctuary. No time of renewal of the people of God has ever occurred apart from a deep sense of conviction of sin and a desire to confess that sinfulness to God and receive his forgiveness.

Returning to the Word of God (22:14–20)

The royal officials sought an instructive word from Yahweh through the prophetess Huldah (22:14). Other prophetic voices were certainly available to them. Jeremiah had begun his prophetic ministry at the time of Josiah's religious reforms (Jeremiah 1:2) and strongly supported them. Zephaniah was also active at this time.

> *God is not limited by ethnic, national, or gender distinctions. . . .*

Could this text's focus on the prophetess Huldah be a reminder that God retains his sovereignty to use any person he desires to use in ministering to others in his name? God is not limited by ethnic, national, or gender distinctions (as we are sometimes). Huldah is not the

Shift in International Power

Josiah was changing Judah, and the world was changing around Josiah. After the death of the Assyrian ruler Ashurbanipal (627 B.C.), the Babylonians (from southern Mesopotamia) under Nabopolassar and the Medes (east of Mesopotamia) under Cyaxares joined their forces against the Assyrian Empire. They destroyed the old capital Ashur (614 B.C.) and the new stronghold Nineveh (612 B.C.).

When the Egyptian pharaoh Neco came to support Assyria, Josiah confronted him in battle at Megiddo and was killed (609 B.C.). Josiah's death was devastating to Judah.

The Babylonians under Nebuchadnezzar (605–562 B.C.) defeated the Egyptians soundly at Carchemish (605 B.C.). Because of the Babylonian victories, the map had changed. Now the land of Israel and Judah was no longer under Assyrian influence but under the shadow of Babylonian power. It was Babylon that interfered in the rule of Josiah's successors until their army besieged Jerusalem. While the Assyrians conquered the Northern kingdom of Israel (722 B.C.), the Babylonians would conquer the Southern kingdom of Judah (586 B.C.) and end the period of the rule of David and his descendants.

---

only woman designated as a prophetess in the Old Testament. Others who served in that ministry role included Miriam (sister of Moses, Exodus 15:20–21), Deborah (the judge or deliverer, Judges 4), and the wife of Isaiah (Isa. 8:3).

Huldah conveyed two divine messages to Josiah. Messenger formulas introduced both of them ("This is what the LORD says," 2 Kings 22:15, 18). The first message declared that God would surely punish Judah for her unfaithfulness to him (22:15–17). The punishment would be the kind of disaster that was contained in the law book that the workers had found in the temple (22:16). This statement reflected the concept that faithfulness would result in the blessing of God, while unfaithfulness would produce his curse or judgment (Deut. 27—28). God would show his anger on sin through his devastating judgment.

> I pray that God will give us the courage to declare our renewed commitment to Jesus and then to act out of that new spirit of dedication.

The second message contained a measure of hope in light of the coming judgment (2 Kings 22:18–20). God would honor the positive responsiveness of Josiah. Although God was going to bring the kingdom of Judah to an end, it would not occur during the reign of Josiah. The language of

1 AND 2 KINGS: Leaders and Followers—Failed and Faithful

The Source of Revival

Most followers of Christ would declare that we need a fresh wind of the blowing of the Holy Spirit. We need spiritual renewal. This kind of religious reformation would require a cooperative effort. From the following list determine the size of the role that each should play (if any) in such a move of God:
- Vocational church leaders
- Government officials
- Denominational leaders
- Teenagers and young adults
- Senior adults
- The laity of the churches

verse 20 describes a peaceful non-violent death. In fact, though, Josiah was killed in battle at Megiddo in 609 B.C. as he tried to prevent the Egyptian army from advancing toward Mesopotamia. At the same time, Josiah died not having to experience the suffering, death, and devastation related to the Babylonian victory over Judah and Jerusalem. In that regard he was "buried in peace" (22:20).

Reviving the People of God (23:1–4)

Josiah received the prophetic word from Huldah and acted decisively in bringing the people together to renew their commitment to God. The summons was inclusive. Josiah invited the citizens of Jerusalem (including royal officials), the tribal leaders from the rural areas, the religious leaders, and ordinary citizens of his kingdom to participate in this time of covenant renewal (23:1–2).

> . . . As we individually renew our heart desires in service to Christ, we will discover we are not alone.

This time of covenant renewal enabled Judah to renew her desire to be a faithful covenant partner to her God. Joshua 24 is a previous example of such a time. On occasions of covenant renewal, a leader reminded the people of the promises they had made to God and encouraged them to recommit themselves to those pledges. Here Josiah served as the covenant mediator (as Moses and Joshua had done on previous occasions).

Josiah stood at a prominent place near the entrance of the temple. "By the pillar" (23:3) seems to suggest that this spot conveyed something about the presence and authority of God. He read the words of the scroll that the remodeling group had found. Josiah pledged to be faithful to God and to obey God completely. The people followed Josiah's positive example. They declared their renewed devotion to God as well.

Josiah asserted his renewed desire to serve God fully and then transformed that assertion into action. He provided leadership for what Israel remembered as the most genuine spiritual reform or revival in the entire period of the kings of Israel and Judah.

The reformation began with the purification of the temple, the place where God himself dwelled in the presence of his people (23:4). Previously Joshua had guided the physical renovation of the building, and now he guided the spiritual renovation. All personnel associated with the temple helped to rid that holy place of all of the idolatrous articles used in fertility worship and astrological practice.

Josiah then destroyed all worship places and dismissed all worship personnel in Jerusalem and Judah that were not part of the pure devotion to Yahweh (23:5–14). He expanded this purification activity to the territory of the Northern kingdom of Israel (23:15–20). In addition to the destruction of improper worship places and furniture, Josiah celebrated Passover (23:21–23) and removed the various practices people had used to receive God's instructions even though God had prohibited them (23:24–25).

If you are willing to serve Jesus faithfully, you will find other people of God standing with you.

Josiah was a great king of Judah, but the spiritual revival was cut short by his untimely death (23:29–30). God honored Josiah's faithfulness, but he would yet fulfill his word of judgment on Judah.

Implications and Actions

Judah had been unfaithful to God, and God promised to judge them. This punishment did not happen during the reign of Josiah because he was sincere in his devotion to God. He had determined to make a difference. God used him as his instrument to bring revival to Judah.

Like Josiah we should be determined to make a difference. I pray that God will give us the courage to declare our renewed commitment to Jesus and then to act out of that new spirit of dedication.

Too, as we individually renew our heart desires in service to Christ, we will discover we are not alone. The World Series hero Bill Mazeroski was not alone. His home run produced only one run of the ten his team scored that day. The hero Josiah was not alone. Laborers found the book. The priest and the royal servant realized its significance and brought it to Josiah. Huldah the prophetess explained what it meant. When Josiah declared his desire to purify the worship of Judah, many others carried out his instructions. If you are willing to serve Jesus faithfully, you will find other people of God standing with you.

QUESTIONS

1. Josiah initiated the physical renovation of the temple, and God directed him toward another kind of renovation, a spiritual one. Someone suggested that God cannot guide or direct us unless we are moving. What do you think of that statement?

2. Josiah had the benefit of both a written resource ("Book of the Law") and a spoken resource (a prophetic word). What are some resources we have today that would help us receive direction from God?

3. Has God ever surprised you in the way he used someone in ministry against all of your expectations? What are some of the ways people tend to limit God as to whom he might want to use in ministering his love to his world?

4. Has it been your experience that when you were willing to stand up boldly for Christ, you discovered that others stood with you? If so, describe that experience.

NOTES

1. Josiah's life is also treated in the priestly history in 2 Chronicles 34—35.

Focal Text
2 Kings 23:31–32, 36–37; 24:8–9, 18–20; 25:8–21

Background
2 Kings 23:31—25:21

Main Idea
God eventually and sometimes swiftly judges people's unfaithfulness.

Question to Explore
Can we trust God to bring justice and call for accountability?

Study Aim
To explain why the events in the destruction of Judah occurred and to draw out principles I will act on today

Study and Action Emphases
- Affirm the Bible as our authoritative guide for life and ministry
- Develop a growing, vibrant faith
- Equip people for servant leadership

LESSON THIRTEEN

The Bitter End

Quick Read
God judged the unfaithfulness of his people through the destruction of Jerusalem. It was a bitter event for Judah.

1 AND 2 KINGS: *Leaders and Followers—Failed and Faithful*

First, let me tell you that I am not an anti-social loner. My wife and I frequently entertain family members and friends in our home. I am happy to greet them when they arrive, but I confess that I am happy to bid them farewell when it is time for them to go. If confession is good for the soul, then here goes. A pet peeve of mine is that some guests will not leave in a timely fashion. The progression follows a typical pattern.

The guests lament that it is getting late, and they really must be getting home. At this point they make no move to support their belief in that statement except to call out to the children upstairs with instructions to get everything picked up. (Going) The conversation continues. Then another hopeful comment is made. They declare their need to get home. This time some adults trudge upstairs to assist the kids in picking up the play room. (Going) That is the beginning of the *standing phase*, when we continue the conversation although we are no longer seated in a comfortable chair. (Going) Slowly but surely we move toward the door, and after continuing the dialogue outside (Going), our guests drive away. (Gone)

Sometimes when it seems that this process is never going to end, I make my legendary statement (not legendary with my wife, I might add). "Wow, it is really late. I would go home, but I live here." I have discovered that this comment is a wonderful textual clue, but I must warn you. It must be said playfully.

The death of good king Josiah (609 B.C.) was a strong indication that Judah's end was not far away (lesson twelve, 2 Kings 22—23). From that time the judgment of God on Judah was certain, but it did not come immediately. Several more kings would come and go before the end came.

Four kings succeeded Josiah and served in an alternating pattern of three months for one and then eleven years for another. They were Jehoahaz (609); Jehoiakim (609–598); Jehoiachin (598/7); and Zedekiah (597–587). None of these kings assumed the throne or served enjoying full independence. During this period Egypt and Babylon competed for influence in Judah's internal affairs.

---

2 Kings 23:31–32, 36–37

31Jehoahaz was twenty-three years old when he became king, and he reigned in Jerusalem three months. His mother's name was Hamutal daughter of Jeremiah; she was from Libnah. **32**He did evil in the eyes of the LORD, just as his fathers had done.

Lesson 13: The Bitter End

⁣⁣⁣⁣⁣⁣⁣⁣⁣⁣

³⁶Jehoiakim was twenty-five years old when he became king, and he reigned in Jerusalem eleven years. His mother's name was Zebidah daughter of Pedaiah; she was from Rumah. ³⁷And he did evil in the eyes of the Lord, just as his fathers had done.

2 Kings 24:8–9, 18–20

⁸Jehoiachin was eighteen years old when he became king, and he reigned in Jerusalem three months. His mother's name was Nehushta daughter of Elnathan; she was from Jerusalem. ⁹He did evil in the eyes of the Lord, just as his father had done.

⁣⁣⁣⁣⁣⁣⁣⁣⁣⁣

¹⁸Zedekiah was twenty-one years old when he became king, and he reigned in Jerusalem eleven years. His mother's name was Hamutal daughter of Jeremiah; she was from Libnah. ¹⁹He did evil in the eyes of the Lord, just as Jehoiakim had done. ²⁰It was because of the Lord's anger that all this happened to Jerusalem and Judah, and in the end he thrust them from his presence.

Now Zedekiah rebelled against the king of Babylon.

2 Kings 25:8–21

⁸On the seventh day of the fifth month, in the nineteenth year of Nebuchadnezzar king of Babylon, Nebuzaradan commander of the imperial guard, an official of the king of Babylon, came to Jerusalem. ⁹He set fire to the temple of the Lord, the royal palace and all the houses of Jerusalem. Every important building he burned down. ¹⁰The whole Babylonian army, under the commander of the imperial guard, broke down the walls around Jerusalem. ¹¹Nebuzaradan the commander of the guard carried into exile the people who remained in the city, along with the rest of the populace and those who had gone over to the king of Babylon. ¹²But the commander left behind some of the poorest people of the land to work the vineyards and fields.

¹³The Babylonians broke up the bronze pillars, the movable stands and the bronze Sea that were at the temple of the Lord and they carried the bronze to Babylon. ¹⁴They also took away the pots, shovels, wick trimmers, dishes and all the bronze articles used in the temple service. ¹⁵The commander of the imperial guard took away the censers and

> sprinkling bowls—all that were made of pure gold or silver. **16**The bronze from the two pillars, the Sea and the movable stands, which Solomon had made for the temple of the LORD, was more than could be weighed. **17**Each pillar was twenty-seven feet high. The bronze capital on top of one pillar was four and a half feet high and was decorated with a network and pomegranates of bronze all around. The other pillar, with its network, was similar.
> **18**The commander of the guard took as prisoners Seraiah the chief priest, Zephaniah the priest next in rank and the three doorkeepers. **19**Of those still in the city, he took the officer in charge of the fighting men and five royal advisers. He also took the secretary who was chief officer in charge of conscripting the people of the land and sixty of his men who were found in the city. **20**Nebuzaradan the commander took them all and brought them to the king of Babylon at Riblah. **21**There at Riblah, in the land of Hamath, the king had them executed. So Judah went into captivity, away from her land.

Going (23:31–32, 36–37)

Josiah's program of religious renewal would have been ten-to-twelve years in duration when he met his untimely death at the hand of the Egyptian pharaoh Neco. The implication of the biblical text is that for the most part the revival died with that good king. Josiah's son Jehoahaz (609 B.C.) succeeded him and received a negative evaluation for doing evil (2 Kings 23:32).

Jehoahaz was not the oldest son of Josiah and thus not in the line of succession to the throne. He may have been placed there by a group that had sympathies toward Babylon. Possibly Neco, the Egyptian ruler, did not consider Jehoahaz to be the legitimate ruler and, after a reign of only three months, removed him from that position. (This three-month rule is confirmed by records discovered by archaeologists at Babylon.) Jehoahaz thus had the distinction of being the first king of Judah ever to be removed from power by a foreign ruler.[1] Neco took Jehoahaz to Egypt (23:33–34). The prophet Jeremiah dashed any hope that Jehoahaz would return from Egypt (Jeremiah 22:11–12), and he later died there. Jeremiah referred to him by his personal name Shallum instead of his throne name Jehoahaz.

Pharaoh Neco was responsible for killing Josiah in battle and for removing his successor Jehoahaz. He then placed his own choice, another son of Josiah, on the throne of Judah. In fact he asserted that Jehoiakim was the successor to Josiah and required him to pay tribute to Egypt (2 Kings 23:34–35).

Jehoiakim (609–598 B.C.) reigned during some of the most crucial years of the kingdom of Judah. The Book of Jeremiah supplies the concrete evidence for the negative evaluation of his reign (23:37). Jehoiakim despised Jeremiah and rejected the many words of divine condemnation delivered to him by this prophet (Jer. 19:3–5; 27:13–19; 36:9–26). Jeremiah preached his great sermon recorded in Jeremiah 7 early in the reign of Jehoiakim, asserting that the temple itself would be destroyed. Jehoiakim responded by trying to have Jeremiah executed for treason (Jer. 26). It was Jehoiakim who imprisoned Jeremiah and burned the scroll he dictated to his assistant Baruch (Jer. 36).

> *He has many modern counterparts who want to know about God but do not want to follow God's purpose and plan for their lives.*

Although the Egyptian king Neco placed Jehoiakim on the throne, Jehoiakim's loyalty went back and forth between Egypt and Babylon (2 Kings 24:1–7). Of course he allied himself with Babylon after Nebuchadnezzar's victory over Egypt at Carchemish in 605 B.C. Several years later he changed his mind again and

Babylonian and Assyrian Resettlement Policies

The experience of the people removed from Israel (722 B.C.) was quite different from that of the ones removed from Judah (598, 586 B.C.). The reason for this was that the Babylonians had a different resettlement policy from that of the Assyrians. The goal of the Assyrians was to reduce any local or regional loyalty that would resist the power of their empire. As a result they moved various people groups out of an area and others into that area, encouraging complete mixing through intermarriage.

The Babylonians seemingly moved carefully-chosen groups of conquered peoples, the ones most capable of leading rebellions in the future. They resettled them in the heart of their empire but allowed them to continue to live in their own ethnic or tribal communities. They did not repopulate conquered areas with people from another place. The exiles from Judah, therefore, maintained their ethnic purity, and some would later return to Judah with Ezra and Nehemiah.

1 AND 2 KINGS: *Leaders and Followers—Failed and Faithful*

The Justice of God

You are on the treadmill doing your aerobic exercise. Two people arrive and interrupt your silence. They are engaged in an intense conversation. You did not hear the beginning of it, but you cannot help but hear where they are in it now. Both of them have become so disturbed about the level of violence and terrorism in the world that they are just about to conclude God does not exist. They agree that if a loving or just God existed, God would certainly do something. What would you say or at least want to say to them?

rebelled against Babylon. As Nebuchadnezzar brought his army toward Judah to deal with this insubordination, Jehoiakim died.

Going (24:8–9, 18–20)

The death of Jehoiakim as Nebuchadnezzar's Babylonian army advanced toward Jerusalem brought his son Jehoiachin (598/7 B.C.) to the throne. The evaluation of his brief three-month reign states that he was no better than his evil father (24:9).

This young king was no match for Babylon. He surrendered himself and his city to Nebuchadnezzar in the turning of the calendar from 598 to 597 B.C. (24:10–12). As a result Jerusalem experienced a partial preview to the final destruction that would come later. The Babylonians took for themselves precious metal from the temple and the king's palace (24:13). They also plundered the wealth of the population. They captured and led away the king, the royal family, royal servants, and skilled craftsmen (24:14–16).

> *Sometimes we may question how long God will put up with consistent unfaithfulness before he decides to punish it.*

Jehoiachin was the last descendant of David who ruled as the legitimate king, that is, who ruled according to the succession process of a son succeeding his father. His successor was his uncle. In the same way that Neco had designated Jehoiakim to be the king of Judah, Nebuchadnezzar designated Mattaniah as the new king and changed his name to Zedekiah (24:17).

Zedekiah (597–87 B.C.) finished the cycle of three months/eleven years for Judah's kings. He was the third son of Josiah to reign over Judah in Jerusalem, but he was more like his brother Jehoiakim in character (24:19).

Judah had been moving toward her bitter end for a number of years. Zedekiah had the misfortune to be the king when she arrived at that sad destination. The language of God's anger as he removed his people from his presence (24:20) is quite similar to that used for the final destruction of the Northern kingdom of Israel (17:18–19).

The final catalyst for Judah's punishment by God was the rebellion of Zedekiah against Babylon (24:20c). Nebuchadnezzar had placed him on Judah's throne, and he responded to this disloyalty with vengeance. Some interpreters contend that Zedekiah's rationale for this rebellion was his hope that the resurgence of Egypt would enable Egypt to compete with Babylon. Jeremiah counseled Zedekiah about the foolishness of depending on Egypt (see Jer. 28).

> We never need to question the reality of God's justice.

Again Jeremiah is helpful in learning more about the character of Zedekiah. The prophet considered this king to be weak and indecisive. Zedekiah frequently sought the counsel of Jeremiah but tragically never seemed to follow his advice (Jer. 21:1–2; 34:1–22). He has many modern counterparts who want to know about God but do not want to follow God's purpose and plan for their lives.

Gone (25:8–21)

Jerusalem and Judah paid a high price for the rebellion of Zedekiah.[2] Nebuchadnezzar surrounded the city and had it under siege for some eighteen months. When the food supply ran out and the Babylonian army breached the walls of the city, the king and his entourage attempted to escape but were not successful (2 Kings 25:3–6).

One month after the Babylonians conquered the city, Nebuzaradan, the Babylonian general, expressed his king's outrage at the rebellion of Zedekiah through his destructive actions. The victors set out to destroy all of the important buildings in Jerusalem by burning the temple and the administrative and residential areas of the king (25:9).

> The question of how long God will put up with someone's sinfulness has within it the conviction that ultimately God will act.

They also tore down the walls that surrounded the city (25:10). This act made the city more vulnerable and created difficulty in attempting to defend the city in the future. (God assigned to Nehemiah the task to rebuild them more than 100 years later.)

The Babylonians used discretion in choosing which people to take into custody and carry into exile and which to leave in Judah. They took what they considered to be the cream of the crop and left "the poorest people of the land" (25:12).

Before the invaders burned down the buildings, they plundered them of their precious ornamental metal and furniture (25:13–17). The focus is on the things Solomon commissioned to be part of his magnificent temple rather than on the ark of the covenant and the rest of the furniture of the tabernacle of Moses. Verses 13–17 should be read alongside 1 Kings 7:15–51, where some of these articles are described more fully. The "bronze pillars" guarded the entrance to the temple, and the "bronze Sea" was a large basin positioned on the back of twelve bulls or oxen, which graced the courtyard of the temple area (2 Kings 25:13).

Nebuzaradan implemented another roundup of prominent citizens, including those who served the king and those who served in the temple (25:18–21). Seraiah was the grandson of Hilkiah, the priest who participated in the revival of Josiah. "Royal advisers" (25:19) translates the phrase *those who saw the king's face*. They were taken to Riblah in Syria and executed in order to serve as an example of what would happen to anyone else who dared to rebel against Babylonian power (25:20). Riblah is also the place where they had taken King Zedekiah. After killing Zedekiah's sons and gouging out his eyes, they took him in chains to Babylon (25:6–7).

> *God promises to punish unfaithfulness to him.*

"So Judah went into captivity, away from her land" (25:21b). The clause is short and simple, but the event was absolutely devastating to the people of God. Judah's last two kings were taken as captives to Babylon. No longer did one of David's sons rule over her as God's representative. In addition to that, Jerusalem, the City of David, lay in almost complete ruin. Of all the buildings in Jerusalem that were leveled, the most significant one to Judah was of course the temple. It had stood for almost 400 years as the place where God had chosen to make his dwelling among his people. Its very presence was evidence for the hope of the Jews. The Book of Lamentations reflects on the overwhelming sadness the people felt as a result of these events.

Lesson 13: The Bitter End

The glory of David and Solomon had ended. Judah had forfeited the right to remain in the land her God had granted to her. He had delivered her from Egyptian slavery. God now judged her by leading her into Babylonian slavery. It was a bitter end to the existence of Judah.

Implications and Actions

Sometimes we may question how long God will put up with consistent unfaithfulness before he decides to punish it. During the period of Judah's history this lesson surveys, the prophet Habakkuk voiced those sentiments. He wondered how long God would put up with the sins of Judah.

> *. . . We should desire to live lives that are faithful to God.*

The question of how long God will put up with someone's sinfulness has within it the conviction that ultimately God will act. He will judge or punish sin. We never need to question the reality of God's justice. God promises to punish unfaithfulness to him. We take God at his word and believe we are accountable to him. We will suffer consequences as a result of our wayward actions.

As a result we should desire to live lives that are faithful to God. We should also allow God the freedom to exercise his judgment in his world according to his way and time.

QUESTIONS

1. Why is it that some children of great spiritual leaders like David, Hezekiah, or Josiah do not share their parents' desire to be faithful to God? What can we do to prevent the experience of that sadness?

2. Why do times of spiritual renewal or revival tend to be short-lived in terms of impact? When God grants a time of genuine Spirit-filled renewal, what can be done from a human perspective to lengthen its influence?

3. How does the destruction of Jerusalem correspond to the New Testament declaration that "it is time for judgment to begin with the family of God" (1 Peter 4:17)?

NOTES

1. Of course, one of his predecessors, Ahaziah (along with Joram the king of Israel), was assassinated by the Israelite Jehu in 842 B.C. (2 Kings 9:14–28).
2. In addition to 2 Kings 25, we also read of the final days of Judah in 2 Chronicles 36:11–21 and Jeremiah 39:1–14; 52:1–34.

Focal Text
Matthew 28:1–10

Background
Matthew 28

Main Idea
Jesus' resurrection can enable us to put away our fear and live with joy and purpose.

Question to Explore
What fears keep you from the joy and purpose God intends for your life?

Study Aim
To recall experiences in which my faith in the resurrected Jesus enabled me to move beyond fear to live with joy and purpose

Study and Action Emphases
- Affirm the Bible as our authoritative guide for life and ministry
- Share the gospel with all people
- Develop a growing, vibrant faith
- Include all God's family in decision-making and service
- Value all people as created in the image of God

EASTER LESSON
"Do Not Be Afraid"

Quick Read
Fear of life or death should not paralyze Christians. We must overcome our fears in order to live in freedom as God intended.

1 AND 2 KINGS: *Leaders and Followers—Failed and Faithful*

I heard shrill screams coming from our house, and I ran to see what had happened. The house in which my wife and I were staying was a small parsonage next door to the church I served while in seminary. On that day, we were cleaning out old papers and useless "stuff" in an unused closet. I had gone out back to put the "stuff" in a trash barrel.

When I heard the screams, my first thought was that a snake (my deepest fear) was in the house. So I grabbed a two-by-four and charged into the living room. My wife was dancing up and down on the couch while screaming, "Mouse! Mouse!" at the top of her lungs.

While I was standing there holding the two-by-four ready to strike, up walked a young couple who had come to the house for pre-marital counseling. Since the front door was open, they saw and heard everything through the screen door. I did my best to reassure them that matters were not as they might be imagining them, but that is not easy to do when one is holding a two-by-four in one's hand and one's wife is screaming. Fortunately, the young couple quickly understood, and the four of us had a great laugh at the absurdity of the scene. The young man aided me in ridding the house of the equally frightened rodent.

What frightens you the most? Nearly all of us have fears. You may be afraid of spiders, snakes, bugs, lizards, mice, public speaking, the dark, a phone call in the middle of the night, flying in an airplane, or death. These fears are only representative of all the things we might fear.

In our Scripture lesson for today, the word "afraid" appears four times. Jesus' resurrection caused fear in the guards at the tomb and in the women who came to the tomb early on Easter Sunday morning. We can receive the same assurance as these women received from the angel: "Do not be afraid. . . . He is not here; he has risen" (Matthew 28:5–6).[1]

The Angel's Appearance (28:1–4)

Joseph of Arimathea and Nicodemus placed Jesus' body in a tomb at dusk on Friday, just before the Sabbath began. The tomb belonged to Joseph and was located near the place where Jesus was crucified. Joseph and Nicodemus were secret believers in Jesus. Both were members of the Jewish Sanhedrin. Nicodemus brought about seventy-five pounds of myrrh and aloes to anoint the body (John 19:38–42). When the men were finished, Mary Magdalene and the other Mary sat and stared at the closed tomb of Jesus (John 27:61). We do not know how long the two of them stayed.

Easter Lesson: "Do Not Be Afraid"

Matthew 28:1–10

¹After the Sabbath, at dawn on the first day of the week, Mary Magdalene and the other Mary went to look at the tomb. ²There was a violent earthquake, for an angel of the Lord came down from heaven and, going to the tomb, rolled back the stone and sat on it. ³His appearance was like lightning, and his clothes were white as snow. ⁴The guards were so afraid of him that they shook and became like dead men.

⁵The angel said to the women, "Do not be afraid, for I know that you are looking for Jesus, who was crucified. ⁶He is not here; he has risen, just as he said. Come and see the place where he lay. ⁷Then go quickly and tell his disciples: 'He has risen from the dead and is going ahead of you into Galilee. There you will see him.' Now I have told you."

⁸So the women hurried away from the tomb, afraid yet filled with joy, and ran to tell his disciples. ⁹Suddenly Jesus met them. "Greetings," he said. They came to him, clasped his feet and worshiped him. ¹⁰Then Jesus said to them, "Do not be afraid. Go and tell my brothers to go to Galilee; there they will see me."

The Jewish leaders requested that Pilate place guards at the tomb's entrance (Matt. 27:62–66). Since Pilate gave the order, we may assume that these were Roman guards.

Before the Easter dawn and the arrival of the women at the tomb, a great earthquake shook the tomb. A similar quake had occurred two days before on the day of Jesus' crucifixion.

An angel from God descended to the tomb's entrance at the same time as the earthquake. The angel rolled the stone away from the tomb's entrance and then sat down on it. The angel's appearance was startling like lightning, with his garments as white as snow. His appearance was like a brilliant flash of light. The biblical account is quite clear that the guards saw the angel.

The earthquake and the angel's appearance were more than the guards could bear. The "fear" expressed by the guards was a natural fear that anyone might experience in the same circumstances. The guards trembled and were as still as dead men. Whether they fell down on the ground or simply stood staring in shock does not matter. Terrified, they fled into the darkness. Later, some of these guards went to the chief priests to report what had happened (28:11–15). The Jewish priests warned them to report only that the disciples of Jesus had stolen the body. The priests paid the soldiers to tell this lie (28:15).

The Angel's Message (28:5–7)

This part of the story is more a report of how Jesus' resurrection was discovered than an account of how he rose from the dead. Bible interpreters often point out that the angel did not roll the stone away in order to let Jesus out. Rather the removal of the stone was so that the world could see Jesus was not there. He rose from the dead. Death and the tomb were not able to hold him.

What frightens you the most?

The women came at dawn to anoint the body. From other Gospel accounts, we know the group of women included Mary Magdalene; Mary the mother of James; Salome; and Joanna (see Mark 16:1 and Luke 24:10). According to the other Gospels, the women also brought more spices. On the way to the tomb, they were discussing how to get the stone rolled aside to enter the burial site (Mark 16:3).

Upon arrival at the tomb, the women found an angel sitting on the stone. Matthew indicates that the women saw the angel in the same bright appearance as the soldiers had (28:3–5). Although the Matthew text does not say specifically that the women were afraid, both Mark 16:5 and Luke 24:5 state they were alarmed.

In an effort to comfort the women, the angel said, "Do not be afraid" (Matt. 28:5). The angel hoped to allay all the fears of the women.

The angel's message shows an awareness of how confusing the event was to the women. The angel knew the women came to the tomb to find Christ still dead. They had no expectations of a resurrection. The angel also knew the tomb was empty. He said, "Come and see the place where he lay."

The Great Commission is a command for every believer.

We know the women did not step forward to see the empty burial site at first because the angel continued his message, "Then go quickly and tell his disciples: 'He has risen from the dead and is going ahead of you into Galilee. There you will see him'" (28:7).

Galilee

Galilee was a region in northern Palestine that was ill-defined until the Roman period. It ran about forty-five miles from north to south. The tribes of Naphtali, Asher, Issachar, and Zebulun occupied the area in the Old Testament. The tribe of Dan later moved to the area. By the time of the first century A.D., a variety of peoples lived in the region. Galilee had the largest concentration of Gentiles of any New Testament Palestine region. Galilee was a wealthy district located on the trade routes between Rome and Egypt and between Syria and the East.

During the time of Jesus, Herod Antipas ruled the territory. With Herod Antipas's banishment by Rome in 39 A.D., Rome gave the district to Herod Agrippa I. After Agrippa's death in 44 A.D., Rome gave the territory to his son Herod Agrippa II, who ruled it until 100 A.D.

Jesus experienced little opposition in the region itself. From this region came eleven of the twelve apostles. Only Judas Iscariot was not from Galilee.

It is interesting to note that the women were the first to hear the announcement of the resurrection. They also were the first people commanded to herald the risen Christ. The gospel message expects every disciple to be a messenger about the good news of the resurrection of Jesus. Matthew 28:19–20 is a command for all disciples—male and female—to "go and make disciples of all nations, baptizing them in the name of the Father and of the Son and of the Holy Spirit, and teaching them to obey everything I have commanded you." This message is not confined to the apostles, and neither is it for only male believers. Men and women make up the church of God. The Great Commission is a command for every believer.

Christians need to remember that God promised to be with us always as we carry out the Great Commission.

The angel added that the disciples should leave Jerusalem and return to Galilee, where they would meet the resurrected Christ. We know from the other Gospels that the disciples must have stayed at least one more week in Jerusalem. Jesus appeared to the apostles on Easter evening and again in the upper room one week later, when Thomas was present (John 20:20–29). Nevertheless, several of his recorded post-resurrection appearances with his disciples occurred in Galilee.

The Appearance of Jesus (28:8–10)

The women responded "with fear and joy" (Matt. 28:8). They did not overcome their fear of seeing a heavenly visitor. It would be difficult for any of us to be calm after such an experience, regardless of reassuring words from an angel. Nevertheless, their "fear" did not paralyze them. They responded to the angel's message to "go quickly." Sometimes our fears keep us from doing what we should do. Christians need to remember that God promised to be with us always as we carry out the Great Commission.

Are we unnecessarily afraid?

Christians are never alone. God is our constant companion. Through Christ, we can do all things (Philippians 4:13). Too, although we may need to do some Christian assignments without a Christian friend, most tasks can use two or more people. A Christian companion makes most godly tasks less intimidating. Seek out a Christian friend to aid you in teaching a class, witnessing to the lost, going on a mission trip, singing the message of God, or helping the poor, sick, and bereaved. Put your fears behind you and know the joy of serving God.

Unexpectedly, the joyful women met Jesus on their way to tell the apostles about the angel's message. The women must have fallen to the ground, for they "clasped his feet" (Matt. 28:9). Jesus used the exact same message to the women which the angel used, "Do not be afraid." He too was gentle in his command.

We must overcome our fears to share the news about the resurrected Jesus with our families, friends, associates at work, and neighbors.

Jesus made himself known first to women. Again, this shows more regard for women than what the Jews normally had. Luke's Gospel—Luke was a Gentile—portrays women in a better light than any other biblical book. God does not show favoritism. We are all one in Christ (Galatians 3:28).

Jesus repeated the angelic message to go and tell the disciples to meet him in Galilee. One possible reason for the instruction was that the apostles and the other disciples would receive less scrutiny in Galilee than in Jerusalem. It was important that the band of disciples remain safe until Jesus could explain his resurrection and its meaning for humankind.

Jesus spent the majority of his earthly ministry in Galilee. Jesus went briefly to Decapolis on the eastern shore of the Sea of Galilee and sometimes to Perea, Jerusalem, and Samaria, but Galilee was his base of operations. All of his apostles—except Judas—were Galileans.

The intermittent appearances of Jesus until his ascension into heaven were filled with instructions for the small band of believers. During this time, the apostles and other disciples became bold in willingness to proclaim the good news. The certainty of the resurrection, along with seeing the resurrected Christ, surely gave power and confidence to all of Jesus' followers. With the arrival of the Holy Spirit on the Day of Pentecost, the apostles were ready to go out with the message of Christ.

Christians today, like the apostles, have the certainty of the resurrection, knowing personally the resurrected Christ and the power of the Holy Spirit in us. What is there to fear? What prevents us from sharing this good news? Are we unnecessarily afraid? We must overcome our fears to share the news about the resurrected Jesus with our families, friends, associates at work, and neighbors. What is the worst that can happen to us if we do? Are we more afraid of what people think of us if we do than what God thinks of us if we do not? Proverbs 1:7 says, "The fear of the Lord is the beginning of understanding." Therefore, let us put aside our fears and spread God's message to all those around us.

> . . . Let us put aside our fears and spread God's message to all those around us.

QUESTIONS

1. What are some things you fear? How do your fears hinder your ability to obey God's call to minister in the name of Christ?

2. What most keeps people from serving God in a Christian ministry? How can these barriers be overcome?

3. What talent has God given you for ministry? In what ways are you using it to serve him?

4. What does the resurrected Jesus' appearance first to women (28:9–10) suggest to you about roles women may play in Christian witness and service?

NOTES

1. Unless otherwise indicated, all Scriptures in this lesson are from the New International Version.

Our Next New Study
(Available for use beginning June 2008)

Growing Together in Christ

UNIT ONE, BEGINNING THE JOURNEY

Lesson 1	Respond to God's Love	John 3:1–16
Lesson 2	Get Together with Fellow Believers	Acts 9:10–19; Romans 12:4–5; Hebrews 10:24–25
Lesson 3	Decide to Live Christ's Way	Mark 8:27–37; Romans 6:1–4

UNIT TWO, GROWING IN CHRIST

Lesson 4	The Discipline of Learning	Matthew 11:28–30; John 14:23–26; 1 Corinthians 3:1–3; Hebrews 5:11–14
Lesson 5	The Discipline of Serving	John 13:3–17
Lesson 6	The Discipline of Giving	2 Corinthians 8:1–9; 9:6–8
Lesson 7	The Discipline of Worship	Mark 1:35–36; Luke 4:16; 11:1–4; Philippians 4:6
Lesson 8	The Discipline of Christlike Relationships	Matthew 18:15–17, 21–35; 2 Corinthians 2:5–11
Lesson 9	The Discipline of Right Living	Colossians 3:1–14

UNIT THREE, GROWING TOGETHER

Lesson 10	Place Priority on Scripture	Acts 2:42; Romans 15:4; 2 Timothy 3:14–17; 2 Peter 1:19–21
Lesson 11	Share Genuine Fellowship	Acts 2:42–47; 1 Corinthians 12:4-11; Philippians 1:3–9
Lesson 12	Worship Together	Acts 2:42–47; 1 Corinthians 11:17–34; Ephesians 5:19–20

1 AND 2 KINGS: *Leaders and Followers—Failed and Faithful*

Lesson 13	Minister to People's Needs	Acts 2:43–45; 3:1–8; 1 Corinthians 16:1–3; James 2:14–17
Lesson 14	Witness to the World	Acts 2:47b; Matthew 28:18–20; John 20:19–21; Acts 11:19–26

Future Adult Bible Studies

For use beginning September 2008

Ephesians, Philippians, Colossians: Living with Faithfulness and Joy

For use beginning December 2008

The Gospel of Matthew: Hope in the Resurrected Christ

How to Order More Bible Study Materials

It's easy! Just fill in the following information. For additional Bible study materials, see www.baptistwaypress.org or get a complete order form of available materials by calling 1-866-249-1799 or e-mailing baptistway@bgct.org.

Title of item	Price	Quantity	Cost
This Issue:			
1 and 2 Kings: Leaders and Followers—Study Guide (BWP001025)	$2.95		
1 and 2 Kings: Leaders and Followers—Large Print Study Guide (BWP001026)	$3.15		
1 and 2 Kings: Leaders and Followers—Teaching Guide (BWP001027)	$3.45		
Additional Issues Available:			
Genesis 12—50: Family Matters—Study Guide (BWP000034)	$1.95		
Genesis 12—50: Family Matters—Large Print Study Guide (BWP000032)	$1.95		
Genesis 12—50: Family Matters—Teaching Guide (BWP000035)	$2.45		
Leviticus, Numbers, Deuteronomy—Study Guide (BWP000053)	$2.35		
Leviticus, Numbers, Deuteronomy—Large Print Study Guide (BWP000052)	$2.35		
Leviticus, Numbers, Deuteronomy—Teaching Guide (BWP000054)	$2.95		
Joshua, Judges—Study Guide (BWP000047)	$2.35		
Joshua, Judges—Large Print Study Guide (BWP000046)	$2.35		
Joshua, Judges—Teaching Guide (BWP000048)	$2.95		
1 and 2 Samuel—Study Guide (BWP000002)	$2.35		
1 and 2 Samuel—Large Print Study Guide (BWP000001)	$2.35		
1 and 2 Samuel—Teaching Guide (BWP000003)	$2.95		
Job, Ecclesiastes, Habakkuk, Lamentations: Dealing with Hard Times—Study Guide (BWP001016)	$2.75		
Job, Ecclesiastes, Habakkuk, Lamentations: Dealing with Hard Times—Large Print Study Guide (BWP001017)	$2.85		
Job, Ecclesiastes, Habakkuk, Lamentations: Dealing with Hard Times—Teaching Guide (BWP001018)	$3.25		
Psalms and Proverbs: Songs and Sayings of Faith—Study Guide (BWP001000)	$2.75		
Psalms and Proverbs: Songs and Sayings of Faith—Large Print Study Guide (BWP001001)	$2.85		
Psalms and Proverbs: Songs and Sayings of Faith—Teaching Guide (BWP001002)	$3.25		
Mark:Jesus' Works and Words—Study Guide (BWP001022)	$2.95		
Mark:Jesus' Works and Words—Large Print Study Guide (BWP001023)	$3.15		
Mark:Jesus' Works and Words—Teaching Guide (BWP001024)	$3.45		
Jesus in the Gospel of Mark—Study Guide (BWP000066)	$1.95		
Jesus in the Gospel of Mark—Large Print Study Guide (BWP000067)	$1.95		
Jesus in the Gospel of Mark—Teaching Guide (BWP000068)	$2.45		
Luke: Journeying to the Cross—Study Guide (BWP000057)	$2.35		
Luke: Journeying to the Cross—Large Print Study Guide (BWP000056)	$2.35		
Luke: Journeying to the Cross—Teaching Guide (BWP000058)	$2.95		
The Gospel of John: The Word Became Flesh—Study Guide (BWP001008)	$2.75		
The Gospel of John: The Word Became Flesh—Large Print Study Guide (BWP001009)	$2.85		
The Gospel of John: The Word Became Flesh—Teaching Guide (BWP001010)	$3.25		
Acts: Toward Being a Missional Church—Study Guide (BWP001013)	$2.75		
Acts: Toward Being a Missional Church—Large Print Study Guide (BWP001014)	$2.85		
Acts: Toward Being a Missional Church—Teaching Guide (BWP001015)	$3.25		
Romans: What God Is Up To—Study Guide (BWP001019)	$2.95		
Romans: What God Is Up To—Large Print Study Guide (BWP001020)	$3.15		
Romans: What God Is Up To—Teaching Guide (BWP001021)	$3.45		

2 Corinthians: Takng Ministry Personally—Study Guide (BWP000008)	$2.35	_____ _____
2 Corinthians: Takng Ministry Personally— Large Print Study Guide (BWP000007)	$2.35	_____ _____
2 Corinthians: Takng Ministry Personally— Teaching Guide (BWP000009)	$2.95	_____ _____
1, 2 Timothy, Titus, Philemon—Study Guide (BWP000092)	$2.75	_____ _____
1, 2 Timothy, Titus, Philemon—Large Print Study Guide (BWP000091)	$2.85	_____ _____
1, 2 Timothy, Titus, Philemon—Teaching Guide (BWP000093)	$3.25	_____ _____
Hebrews and James—Study Guide (BWP000037)	$1.95	_____ _____
Hebrews and James—Teaching Guide (BWP000038)	$2.45	_____ _____
Revelation—Study Guide (BWP000084)	$2.35	_____ _____
Revelation—Large Print Study Guide (BWP000083)	$2.35	_____ _____
Revelation—Teaching Guide (BWP000085)	$2.95	_____ _____

Coming for use beginning June 2008

Growing Together in Christ—Study Guide (BWP001036)	$3.25	_____ _____
Growing Together in Christ—Large Print Study Guide (BWP001037)	$3.55	_____ _____
Growing Together in Christ—Teaching Guide (BWP001038)	$3.75	_____ _____

Standard (UPS/Mail) Shipping Charges*	
Order Value	Shipping charge
$.01—$9.99	$6.00
$10.00—$19.99	$7.00
$20.00—$39.99	$8.00
$40.00—$79.99	$9.00
$80.00—$99.99	$12.00
$100.00—$129.99	$14.00
$130.00—$149.99	$18.00
$150.00—$199.99	$21.00
$200.00—$299.99	$26.00
$300.00 and up	10% of order value

Cost of items (Order value) _____

Shipping charges (see chart*) _____

TOTAL _____

*Plus, applicable taxes for individuals and other taxable entities (not churches) within Texas will be added. Please call 1-866-249-1799 if the exact amount is needed prior to ordering.

Please allow three weeks for standard delivery. For express shipping service: Call 1-866-249-1799 for information on additional charges.

_____

YOUR NAME   PHONE

_____

YOUR CHURCH   DATE ORDERED

_____

MAILING ADDRESS

_____

CITY   STATE   ZIP CODE

MAIL this form with your check for the total amount to
BAPTISTWAY PRESS, Baptist General Convention of Texas,
333 North Washington, Dallas, TX 75246-1798
(Make checks to "Baptist Executive Board.")

OR, **FAX** your order anytime to: 214-828-5376, and we will bill you.

OR, **CALL** your order toll-free: 1-866-249-1799
(M-Th 8:30 a.m.-8:30 p.m.; Fri 8:30 a.m.-5:00 p.m. central time),
and we will bill you.

OR, **E-MAIL** your order to our internet e-mail address:
baptistway@bgct.org, and we will bill you.

OR, **ORDER ONLINE** at www.baptistwaypress.org.

We look forward to receiving your order! Thank you!